THE PURITAN ETHIC AND WOMAN SUFFRAGE

The Puritan Ethic

AND

Woman Suffrage

ALAN P. GRIMES

NEW YORK

OXFORD UNIVERSITY PRESS

1967

6510

For M.S.G.

CONTENTS

INTRODUCTION

First came the trappers into the mountains in search of beaver, following the waters of the North Platte into what became Wyoming, the South Platte into Colorado, the Green into Utah, the Snake into Idaho. Then came the miners in search of gold and silver; next came the ranchers with their herds of sheep and cattle, and the farmers, the planters of wheat, beets, and potatoes which would sustain them all. They took the bounty of the frontier, animal, mineral, and vegetable. In time came the railroads, following the early trails. Within the space of little more than a generation statehood followed permanent settlement.

Who could have anticipated that woman suffrage would come out of this remote and rugged Rocky Mountain region? Yet only in Wyoming, Utah, Colorado, and Idaho was the modern American woman suffrage movement successful in the nineteenth century. Early in the twentieth century the states west of the Rockies adopted woman suffrage, so that by the time Congress proposed the Nineteenth Amendment, woman suffrage was as much a regional phenomenon of the West as the white primary was of the South. Why was woman suffrage so successful in the West? How may we account for this civilized and sophisticated extension of the suffrage along the last frontier? This book offers an answer to such queries.

The extension of the franchise to women coincided with a fundamental change in social values concerning the role of women in American life. It must not be overlooked that it took the votes of men to enfranchise women, as today it has taken the votes of whites to bring meaningful suffrage to Negroes in the South. Such grants of the ballot are not made without some considerations of political self-interest on the part of the grantors. What kind of America did supporters of woman suffrage expect to develop through the enfranchisement of women? What social values were promised, which constituencies supported woman suffrage, and who in turn was threatened by this change in the electorate?

Woman suffrage, like its companion movement prohibition, has presented difficulties of analysis because it did not arise from clearly defined economic interests; further, again like prohibition, the issue of woman suffrage involved a status conflict which was inevitably interlaced with a conflict over values. Several studies have shown the relevance of status conflict to the prohibition issue; [1] I have undertaken a somewhat similar analysis here of woman suffrage.

If we look beyond the issue of equal rights for women and inquire as to who in America thought they would gain power if women voted, and who thought they would lose power, we get to the substantive issues with which this book is concerned. Struggling for power and status behind the relatively innocuous phrase of equal rights for women were social forces whose ultimate goal was the establishment of a system of values embedded in the law. Many of the values which triumphed are accepted today without question, if not always honored in fact—restrictions on child labor, regulations concerning the conditions of work for women, equal pay for women for equal work, etc. Other of the values once associated with woman suffrage have since been prohibited or repealed—polygamy in Utah, prohibition, and the national origins system of immigration.

In part, my interest in the background of woman suffrage in America arose out of an effort to explain a paradox: in 1869 the modern woman suffrage movement was formally launched in the East with the establishment of the National Woman Suffrage Association and the American Woman Suffrage Association; yet it was in that year in remote, primitive Wyoming Territory that woman suffrage was first enacted into law, followed three months later by a similar enactment in the Mormon Territory of Utah. Why did the actuality of woman suffrage come out of the West when the ideology of the movement came out of the East? Was woman suffrage, then, a demonstration of frontier equality? Or was it, perhaps, a response to the general shortage of women in the frontier settlements, a kind of political bait to lure women from the East? Yet in Utah the ratio of women to men was approximately equal. Economic factors do not appear significant in the western woman suffrage movement, for there was a smaller percentage of women gainfully employed outside the home there than elsewhere in the country. Why was it easy to get rurally oriented state legislatures to authorize referenda on woman suffrage and next to impossible (only nine times out of forty-one elections) to get a popular majority to endorse it? Clearly there were deep-seated conflicts over the issue of social control which have at times been hidden by the often inspired rhetoric of the woman suffrage supporters.

Finally, it should be observed that an issue which provokes students fifty years later to wonder why there was ever a conflict on the subject provides an opportunity objectively to relate values articulated to votes cast, to find a social basis for social attitudes. Changes in the structure of political power are usually associated with changes in social values. What is evident today in the civil rights movement may thus be seen as equally relevant in the era which brought about woman suffrage. By analyzing the votes of Congress on issues involving what may be termed correlative values, that is, values which tended to be held by those who supported woman suffrage, we may see what kinds of constituencies supported the enfranchisement.

"In an important sense," James H. Baker, the president emeritus of the University of Colorado noted in 1927, "Puritan standards have become the public standards of America, and you will find more of New England in Colorado Springs, Boulder, or Greeley than in most towns of Massachusetts. This is not a partisan claim, but recognition of a fact." [2] The following study, in general, supports this conclusion.

Perhaps a word is in order as to what is not attempted or intended in what follows. This is not in any sense a history of woman suffrage; [3] nor is it a study of the ideas of the leadership of the movement; [4] nor is my emphasis on correlative values intended as a subtle suggestion that many of the persons involved in the suffrage movement were anything less than sincere and dedicated to the cause of equal political rights for women. I am, however, arguing that the evidence indicates that to a large extent, at least in the West, the constituency granting woman suffrage was composed of those who also supported prohibition and immigration restriction and felt woman suffrage would further their enactment. Because the woman suffrage movement arose and developed in the West, my study has dealt primarily with this region; it has been in this region, moreover, that research on the topic has been most neglected.

I am indebted to many for assistance on this manuscript: to Janet Winger, Susan Shull, and Douglas Morgan, among others, for assistance with the research; to my colleague Joseph A. Schlesinger, for patiently and critically hearing me expound the thesis herein, and helping me construct the tables in Chapter 6; to my wife, Margaret W. Grimes, for exercising judicious editorial severity; and to Mrs. Anthony Williams, for typing. All are absolved from whatever faults may follow.

A. P. G.

East Lansing
January 1967

THE PURITAN ETHIC AND WOMAN SUFFRAGE

CHAPTER I

Frontier Equalitarianism and Woman Suffrage

The gifts of fortune are promised in the West and
to the West they bend their course.

Alexis de Tocqueville

It has been nearly a century since Wyoming Territory
pioneered with woman suffrage in 1869, nearly half a century since the Nineteenth Amendment was ratified in
1920. A political and social movement which was once the
cause of placards and parades, street demonstrations and
civic commotion, now rates only a passing paragraph in
conventional histories. But to the social and political
theorist some nagging questions remain to be answered
about the greatest enfranchisement in our history.

Every acquisition of political rights by one group
affects the distribution of power held by others. Lurking
behind the avowed principles of justice and eternal right
are conflicts of interests and struggles for power out of
which the law emerges with its affirmation of social values.
When questions of the extension of the franchise are at
issue it is never forgotten that potential voters are potential sources of power in the community, and how they
might utilize this power becomes of great concern to the
voters who must decide upon their enfranchisement. What
would seem so readily evident when applied to other ex-

tensions of the vote—the elimination of property qualifications for voting, for example, or the elimination of racial barriers—has remained largely unexamined in the enfranchisement of women, but surely here too there were political interests in conflict and social values at stake. Surely here too there was a functional or instrumental aspect to the issue of enfranchisement, in which avowed rights, articulated interests, and the social goals to be attained pointed to the enforcement of a set of social values. It is the intention of this study to explore the functional aspect of the woman suffrage issue; not to treat these political ideas as abstract conceptions, but to search for the social constituency which underlay them and which sought to enact social values into the law of the land.

*

What has made the full implications of the woman suffrage movement in the United States difficult to fathom has been its complexity, its interrelatedness to a host of other social values. In this complexity it was unlike most other extensions of the franchise which brought the right to vote to fairly well-defined minorities—racial, religious, propertyless—of generally determinate (low) socioeconomic status. The advocates of woman suffrage proposed a massive extension of the franchise to a potential majority which ultimately cut through all classes, religions, races, and national origins. Politically, the results would be tantamount to a gigantic two-for-one, across-the-board stock split for married voters.

From the formal beginnings of the woman suffrage movement at Seneca Falls in 1848, the cause was intertwined with antislavery and temperance crusades as well as with the broader issues of women's rights in society generally. The feminist movement of the nineteenth century, like the civil rights movement today, sponsored not only immediate reforms benefiting its own group such as the right of women to enter the universities and the professions, to hold property, and to have custody of their children in divorce cases, but also a host of broader reforms such as peace, temperance, abolition of slavery, and the beginnings of social welfare legislation. In this broad assault upon the felt evils of the times the woman suffrage movement both contributed to and in return reflected a new ethic—or an old one revitalized—of civility and reason supplanting the traditional rule of force and brute strength in society. Like the civil rights movement today, this was not an isolated American experience, for similar and parallel woman suffrage movements took place at roughly the same time in the Scandinavian countries, in England, New Zealand, and Australia. Was it that in some vague Hegelian sense the time was ripe for woman suffrage in some parts of the world? If so, why?

There may be some merit in proceeding from a general analysis to a more particular one in order to see the broad issue of social values in question in proper perspective. With this approach we may hypothesize that the late nineteenth-century woman suffrage movement was driven forward by a necessity contained within broad historical forces. For example, it may be argued that the movement was a necessary consequence of the democratic and equalitarian ethic which would in time produce its harvest of universal adult suffrage. "All eyes are opened, or opening, to the rights of man," Jefferson had proclaimed shortly before his death.[1] Could it not be expected that, before long, women would enjoy these rights? "A government of equal rights must, therefore, rest upon mind; not wealth, not brute force, the sum of moral intelligence of the community should rule the State," the historian George Bancroft had noted in an early essay.[2] Would not, in time, the crude democracy which had struggled with savages along the frontier and erected bustling harbors and prosperous cities along the coast, be supplanted by a refined democracy guided by moral intelligence, in which women had equal voice? If the wave of the future inevitably brought forth democratic achievement and equalitarian goals, then Tocqueville, for all his forebodings, saw this course most presciently.

> In perusing the pages of our history, we shall scarcely meet with a single great event, in the lapse of seven hundred years, which has not turned to the advantage of equality. The Crusades and the wars of the English decimated the nobles and divided their possessions; the erection of communities introduced an element of democratic liberty into the bosom of feudal monarchy; the invention of firearms equalized the villain and the noble on the field of battle; printing opened the same resources to the minds of all classes; the post was organized so as to bring the same information to the door of the poor man's cottage and to the gate of the palace; and Protestantism proclaimed that all men are alike able to find the road to heaven. The discovery of America offered a thousand new paths to fortune, and placed riches and power within the reach of the adventurous and the obscure.[3]

Both the pen and the sword, learning and gunpowder; both theology and economics, Protestantism and capitalism; both domestic tranquillity and international holocaust—all conspired, wittingly or unwittingly, to further the cause of democratic equalitarianism:

> All have been blind instruments in the hands of God.
> . . . The gradual development of the equality of condi-

tions is therefore a providential fact, and it possesses all the characteristics of a Divine decree: it is universal, it is durable, it constantly eludes all human interference, and all events as well as all men contribute to its progress.[4]

Tocqueville was, of course, referring to the collapse of the system of status relationships which had so characterized historic European feudalism, but his analysis was so comprehensive that it might equally apply to all other barriers of class. Long before the seminal writing of Max Weber, Tocqueville had had a glimmering of the interconnection of Protestantism, capitalism, and democracy, and had seen in America the substantive result of these interdependent forces at work. Having seen in democratic equalitarianism the necessity of history together with the presence of divine decree, Tocqueville predicted that the social conditions of the Anglo-Americans in the New World would drive them to a further realization of political equality as well: "To conceive of men remaining forever unequal upon one single point, yet equal on all others, is impossible; they must come in the end to be equal upon all." [5] This historical evolution toward political equality, he believed, would ultimately eventuate in universal manhood suffrage without property restrictions on voting.

> When a nation modifies the elective qualification, it may easily be foreseen that sooner or later that qualification will be entirely abolished. There is no more invariable rule in the history of society: the further electoral rights are extended, the greater is the need of extending them; for after each concession the strength of the democracy increases, and its demands increase with its strength.[6]

When Tocqueville wrote, it was too early in the nineteenth century for him to be aware of what would become the woman's rights movement; yet there was nothing in the logic of his historical necessity which would restrict the realization of equal rights to adult men alone. If Protestantism was a mighty historical force conducive to the rise of equalitarianism—and it was in the Protestant countries that the woman suffrage movement was most successful—it must eventually break through the status barriers of sex. Alternatively, if economic independence was the key factor in the rise of equalitarianism, one might expect the rise of woman's rights movements wherever there was a high percentage of women gainfully employed outside the home. Despite his perspicuity and prescience, Tocqueville was himself a product of the early nineteenth century and saw in sex distinctions insurmountable barriers to the acquisition of equal political rights. Still, he came remarkably close to that basic insight which would have carried him on to see the Puritan logic behind woman suffrage.

No free communities ever existed without morals; and . . . morals are the work of women. Consequently, whatever affects the condition of women, their habits, and their opinions, has great political importance in my eyes. Among almost all Protestant nations young women are far more mistresses of their own actions than they are in Catholic countries. This independence is still greater in Protestant countries like England, which have retained or acquired the right of self-government; the spirit of freedom is then infused into the domestic circle by political habits and by religious opinions. In the United States the doctrines of Protestantism are combined with great political freedom and a most democratic state of society; and nowhere are young women surrendered so early or so completely to their own guidance.[7]

For all that the Americans were a religious people, they had equipped their women with the armament of reason, he believed. Would not therefore the very forces of democracy which had destroyed other forms of inequality "ultimately affect that great inequality of man and woman which has seemed, up to the present day, to be eternally based in human nature? I believe that the social changes which bring nearer to the same level the father and son, the master and servant, and superiors and inferiors generally speaking, will raise woman and make her more and more the equal of man." [8] Yet, having gathered up the momentous forces of history for a span of more than seven hundred years and brought them into focus in the emerging American society, Tocqueville concluded lamely that Nature's differentiation of the sexes was made for a profounder purpose than could be encompassed within a simple equalitarian ethic—and this the Americans wisely realized: "The Americans have applied to the sexes the great principle of political economy which governs the manufactures of our age, by carefully dividing the duties of man from those of woman, in order that the great work of society may be the better carried on." [9] At this point Tocqueville's comprehensive grasp of historical necessity succumbed to the conventions of the nineteenth century.

*

As we have seen, one of the most fundamental decisions a society may make is that which determines the composition of the eligible electorate. In a democracy it is a decision made by an existing majority, or in its name, which may determine the composition of a future majority. It is a decision therefore which may serve as some index to prevailing social values. In Tocqueville's day, and indeed until the passage of the Fourteenth Amendment, it was evident that the prevailing social consensus saw the political community as being composed of white, adult, male citizens. Extensions of the suffrage were commonly thought of within the context of the white male community. Although the logic of democratic history propelled society toward the realization of universal adult suffrage, prior to the Civil War it was clear that the equalitarian ethic could not overcome the barriers of race and sex. Negroes in fact lost ground politically during the same historical period that saw such vast extensions of the vote to white adult males, even including in some states resident aliens. Only in six states—Maine, Massachusetts, New Hampshire, Vermont, Rhode Island, and New York—were Negroes not prohibited from voting prior to the Civil War. In six other states constitutional changes had been enacted to prevent Negroes from voting (Delaware, 1792; Kentucky, 1799; Maryland, 1809; Connecticut, 1818; New Jersey, 1820; Pennsylvania, 1838).[10] Putting aside the southern states, where, of course, Negroes could not vote prior to the Fourteenth Amendment, in all of the fifteen remaining states from Ohio west to California Negroes were excluded from the suffrage by law. If there was such a thing as frontier equalitarianism, at this time it was clearly applicable only to white, adult males.

There is an instructive parallel in looking at woman suffrage in conjunction with Negro suffrage. It was not only that both issues became politically significant at the close of the Civil War, nor that in a sense they were competing movements to broaden the electorate. The striking parallel is the obvious one: color and sex mark conspicuous differences. As long as suffrage qualifications dealt only with white, adult males, there were no conspicuous differences in the electorate at the polling booths and it was possible to reduce the qualifications for voting without making apparent a significant difference. Prevailing social values, rather than abstract political theorizing about freedom or inherent rights, determined the composition of the electorate. Even as expediency more than principle governed the determination of the franchise prior to the Civil War, so, it seems reasonable to expect, was the case following the Civil War. Matters of race and sex were extrinsic, so to speak, to democratic-equalitarianism which dealt intrinsically with the political representation of white, adult males. If nonwhites, or women, were to gain equal political status with white, adult males, prevailing social and political assumptions would have to be changed. Abstract principles have always been interpreted in terms of prevailing political values. As Kirk Porter, in his *History of Suffrage in the United States* (1918), noted:

> If these arguments [about abstract democratic principles] were taken seriously they would lead to a startling conclusion when traced back through the pages of this book. The women said that there was no democracy if they did not have the ballot. Ten years before the free negroes [sic] said the same about themselves, but the women were scarcely thought of then. About that time the same thing was said in order to aid the cause of the thrifty aliens who were taxed and governed without their consent, but the women and negroes [sic] were not considered. A few years earlier the non-taxpaying prolitariat said the same thing about themselves, but had no thought of the women, the aliens, and the negroes [sic]. Farther back still, when even the small taxpayer was excluded, he shouted the same thing to the property owners, who alone enjoyed the suffrage. What an unspeakable despotism must have existed in the days of Washington and Jefferson.[11]

Because in practice American democracy was generally restricted to whites in the nineteenth century, it was not thought either feasible or desirable to extend the franchise to Negroes through the normal political process of state constitutional amendment. Indeed from the conclusion of the Civil War until the ratification of the Fifteenth Amendment in 1870 white majorities defeated referendums intended to grant the franchise to Negroes in the states of Connecticut, Wisconsin, Minnesota, Kansas, and New York, in Colorado Territory, and in the District of Columbia. Only in Iowa, and in a third referendum in Minnesota, did Negro suffrage ultimately prevail at the polls; these victories probably brought the franchise to fewer than a thousand Negroes. Where popular referendums failed to do so, the Fifteenth Amendment, guided by congressional Republicans, brought the franchise to Negroes. They, in turn, were expected to bring Republicans to Congress. Nor was this factor of expediency unnoticed by the Democratic majorities in the state legislatures of California, Deleware, Kentucky, Maryland, Oregon, Tennessee, and Ohio which refused to ratify the Fifteenth Amendment. It took the aid of the Republican-controlled Reconstruction governments in the South to accomplish the ratification of the Fifteenth Amendment. So intransigent was the belief in white superiority in post-Civil War America that by 1918, virtually on the eve of the woman suffrage amendment, the Fifteenth Amendment was accepted in many quarters as a dead letter. For example, Kirk Porter found that in the period between the Civil War and World War I "two great conspicuous suffrage movements went forward side by side: (1) the expansion of the suffrage to include the women, and (2) the disfranchising of the negro." In sum, Porter observed, "the cause of negro suffrage is well-nigh lost and bids fair not to be revived again." [12]

When it was revived in the 1960's, it was as much because Negro votes were needed as because Negroes needed votes. Could there be a useful parallel here to help explain the coming of woman suffrage?

*

Today, woman suffrage is all but universal; nearly one hundred countries provide for woman suffrage in national elections, 65 of them just since the end of World War II. What becomes apparent, however, in reviewing the growth of woman suffrage around the world is that in most instances it took place in the wake of phenomenal circumstances. It came about in much of the world with the rise to independent status of new political communities. It was, thus, a product of revolutionary—peaceful or otherwise—political change. For example, Israel adopted woman suffrage in 1948; India and Indonesia did likewise in 1949, Ghana in 1950, Chad, Dahomey, Mali, and Senegal in 1956. For older nations, it was the cataclysm of war which precipitated the social changes necessary to produce woman suffrage. The political settlements following World War II brought about woman suffrage in France, Italy, Japan, Hungary, Albania, and Yugoslavia; the political consequences of World War I affected the coming of woman suffrage to Austria, Czechoslovakia, Germany, Poland, Canada, the Netherlands and, indeed, the USSR and the United States. The twentieth century has been the century of woman suffrage, and in large measure war has been the catalyst which has hastened the advent of this benign result.

Prior to World War I, only four countries had adopted woman suffrage: New Zealand (1893), Australia (1902), Finland (1906), and Norway (1913). In the United

States, by the end of 1914, eleven states had adopted woman suffrage: Wyoming (1890), Colorado (1893), Utah (1896), Idaho (1896), Washington (1910), California (1911), Oregon (1912), Arizona (1912), Kansas (1912), Nevada (1914), and Montana (1914). There is a pattern here and an apparent paradox. The pattern reveals the origin of woman suffrage along what may be loosely called the new frontiers of democracy: the Protestant perimeters of Europe; English-speaking outposts, and the last settlements of America. The paradox is found when it is noted that the ideological wellsprings for the woman suffrage movement were in London, not Christchurch or Sidney; in Rochester, New York, and Boston, not Cheyenne, Salt Lake City, or Denver. The sources of the ideology and the political movements did not coincide. The social and economic preconditions of ideological enterprise and ingenuity in the cause of American woman suffrage were the civilities and sophistication of the advanced state of culture found in the mature societies of the eastern states. Yet it was the comparatively primitive and undeveloped states of the West that first adopted woman suffrage. By 1914, eleven of the last eighteen states admitted into the Union had statewide woman suffrage; none of the first thirty states in the Union had accomplished this. According to the authoritative *Woman Suffrage and Politics* by Carrie Chapman Catt and Nettie Shuler, between 1870 and 1910 there had been in the United States 480 campaigns in 33 states to secure the submission of state woman suffrage amendments to voters.[13] Yet from this activity only 17 referendums in some 11 states had resulted, with successes in only Colorado and Utah. But it is important to note that 14 of these 17 referendums were held in states west of the Mississippi, thus indicating a greater willingness on the part of western state legislatures to submit this question to the voters. Clearly, in the United States, the woman suffrage movement was strongest in the West in the nineteenth century. Was this due, perhaps, to frontier equalitarianism?

*

Ever since the period of the French Revolution, Frederick Jackson Turner noted (in an article published in 1903), "there has been an inclination on the part of writers on democracy to emphasize the analytical and theoretical treatment to the neglect of the underlying factors of historical development." In seeking to understand structural changes in the political system, he counseled, we must understand that in effecting these changes "both conscious ideals and unconscious social reorganization are at work."

> The careful student of history must, therefore, seek the explanation of the forms and changes of political institutions in the social and economic forces that determine them. . . . These are the vital forces that work beneath the surface and dominate the external form. It is to changes in the economic and social life of a people that we must look for the forces that ultimately create and modify organs of political action.[14]

In his search for the underlying social and economic forces, Turner turned to the basic conditions and circumstances of frontier life. It had been the presence in America of a frontier of free lands, he wrote, that had "promoted individualism, economic equality, freedom to rise, democracy." [15] It had been the presence of frontier democracy that had in effect forced upon the eastern communities extensions of the franchise in the early periods of our history.

It was *western* New York that forced an extension of suffrage in the constitutional convention of that State in 1821; and it was *western* Virginia that compelled the tidewater region to put a more liberal suffrage provision in the constitution framed in 1830, and to give to the frontier region a more nearly proportionate representation with the tide-water aristocracy. . . .[16]

It was always implicit in the Turner thesis that long-settled or mature societies tended, perhaps inevitably, to develop rigid lines of social stratification. By way of contrast, frontier society, in the fullness of its youthful exuberance and buoyant optimism, its energy and its activity, had neither the need nor the temperament for social distinctions. One need not resort to the abstract theorizing of a Locke or even a Jefferson to understand the equalitarian ethic in a state of nature; one need only observe the conditions of life along the American frontier.

Western innovation could thus be compared with eastern stability, whether or not one concurred with Turner's hyperbole: "American democracy is fundamentally the outcome of the experiences of the American people in dealing with the West." [17] Probably the strongest statement of such a western thesis was that presented by Walter Prescott Webb in *The Great Plains* (1931). Perhaps the explanation for the origins of woman suffrage in the American West lies in the Webb study. Comprehending under the term "the Great Plains" all territory west of the ninety-eighth meridian (roughly, a vertical line dropped from Grand Forks, North Dakota, which passes through Austin, Texas), Webb argued that the natural environmental characteristics—comparatively level surface, treeless land, subhumid climate—made this area a distinctive region with distinctive social and political characteristics.

While the ax, the boat, and the rifle had been useful instruments for conquering the frontier east of the ninety-eighth meridian, barbed wire, the windmill, and the Colt revolver had been essential instruments in the taming of the Great Plains. The frontiersman of James Fenimore Cooper's novels, for instance, used to tramping through lush forest trails with fresh water close at hand, would have found himself ill prepared to cope with the vast, arid, open plains, the high plateaus that stretched, seemingly forever, westward. "The failure to recognize the fact," Webb wrote, "that the Plains destroyed the old formula of living and demanded a new one led the settlers into disaster, the lawmakers into error, and leads all who will not see into confusion." [18]

Turner's view of frontier conditions as a social influence, interacting politically with the stable and conservative impulses emanating from the seaboard societies, pulling them along the path of democracy, was still essentially eastern in both its scope and application. It was a frontier thesis of fertile plains and shaggy forests and river valleys.[19] Webb's thesis, on the other hand, dealt essentially with the West of the post-Civil War era, a Texan's West of cattle kingdoms, railroads, and dry farming. It is, like Turner's frontier, a preindustrial conception, curiously unconcerned with the place of gold, silver, and oil in fashioning the politics of the region. Like W. J. Cash's classic, *The Mind of the South,* Webb's *The Great Plains* sought a thematic explanation for a variety of phenomena, one that would make intelligible "in a way that no other view has, those very phenomena which give Western life and institutions their singularly unique and elusive character." [20] It was an explanation at once both sensible and simple: "That our [Great Plains] civilization and methods of pioneering were worked out east of the ninety-eighth meridian and were well suited to conditions there, but that when these institutions of the East undertook to cross into the Great Plains they broke down and had to be modified." [21] In Webb's view, the vast, semiarid, sparsely populated cattle ranges produced a distinctive breed of western man, the genuine cowboy: hardy, courageous, and self-reliant.

> A process of natural selection went on in the cattle country as it probably did nowhere else on the frontier. It worked there for a longer time, owing to the pause of the frontier on the edge of the Plains, and it has resulted in a rather distinctive Western psychology. Along with selection went rapid and willing adaptation, which is merely a part of natural selection. If the general thesis here set forth is true, that men had to give up old methods and adopt new ones when they crossed the ninety-eighth meridian, then it would follow that only those who were willing to do this and to do it rapidly would survive in the new environment.[22]

Webb's West was, quite literally, white man's country, and specifically Anglo-Saxon, at that. His natural selection applied within the ranks of native-born Americans; his concept of the Great Plains suggests almost a mountain fastness of Anglo-Saxondom secure against the encirclement of outsiders. "The Negroes did not move west of the ninety-eighth meridian, the Europeans were not attracted by the arid lands, the Chinese remained on the Pacific coast, and the Mexican element stayed close to the southern border." Germans and Scandinavians had settled along the plains of the Midwest, in Illinois, Iowa, the Dakotas and Montana. "But once we go into the arid region of the Plains, particularly in the Southwest, we find, or did find until very recent times, the pure American stock—Smiths, Joneses, McDonalds, Harveys, Jameses, and so on." [23] The West was not only white man's country, but a young man's country. It was a land of glamour and romance, yet one requiring the rugged utmost of men in stamina, fortitude, courage, enterprise, and endurance. The distances were great, the population sparse, and women a scarcity. "The result was that they [women] were very dear and were much sought after, prized, and protected by every man. The men fitted into the Plains; the life appealed to them, especially to those who were young and in good health. But the Plains—mysterious, desolate, barren, grief-stricken— oppressed the women, drove them to the verge of insanity in many cases, as the writers of realistic fiction have recognized." [24]

How, then, may we account for the coming of woman suffrage first to the West—to Wyoming and Utah, to Colorado and Idaho? Had a special breed of western women developed by a process of natural selection to match their rugged male counterparts; were they intrepid innovators, political Amazons, who would not be denied the ballot? Instead of natural selection, had a natural law of supply and demand operated to place such a high premium on the scarce commodity, women, that special inducements were required to bring it into adequate supply? Was woman suffrage such an inducement? Or was the social ecology of the late nineteenth-century West such that it made for a basic kind of equalitarianism, that it overthrew the conventional political distinctions of sex? Webb, aware of the problem presented by woman suffrage, hints at some of the above hypotheses yet leaves the question undecided.

Why the men of the West were the first to grant the women the franchise is a problem that remains to be

solved. Its final solution will grow out of a better under-
standing of a peculiar psychology which developed in a
region where population was sparse and women were
comparatively scarce and remarkably self-reliant. It was
not the vaunted chivalry of the South nor the cool justice
of the Brahman of the North that gave women the ballot.
There is hidden somewhere in the cause the spirit of the
Great Plains which made men democratic in deed and in
truth.[25]

*

Tocqueville, Turner, and Webb, diverse as they were in
their interests and orientations, had in common an awareness that in some fashion the American frontier was related to the democratic ethic. In Tocqueville's day, the
New World marked in a sense the frontier of European
civilization; it was an outpost in Arcadia. The European
migration was but the beginning of a seemingly endless
journey for the generations of man.

> Thus the European leaves his cottage for the transatlantic
> shore; and the American, who is born on that very coast,
> plunges in his turn into the wilds of central America.
> This double emigration is incessant; it begins in the re-
> motest parts of Europe, it crosses the Atlantic Ocean, and
> it advances over the solitudes of the New World. Millions
> of men are marching at once toward the same horizon;
> their languages, their religion, their manners differ, their
> object is the same. The gifts of fortune are promised in
> the West, and to the West they bend their course.[26]

If the search for fortune was the common goal, the methods of attaining it were matters of dispute, as were questions concerning the kinds of society in which the search
should take place. Indeed, woman suffrage was a by-

product of disputes over these fundamental social questions.

Since woman suffrage came first along the frontiers of civilization, it is to these outposts in America that we must turn to find that convenient combination of factors and forces which made this extraordinary development possible. And it was extraordinary within the context of the frontier and the style of life associated with it. It seems almost a trick of history, like the arrival of Marxism in the least developed rather than the most advanced industrial societies. Woman suffrage, a sophisticated, advanced political concept, first became law in America not in the mellowed political societies of the seaboard states, but in the primitive territory of a new frontier, Wyoming (1869) which was itself but a few months old in its territorial status; and in Utah (1870), which was truly unique as a society not only in the West but in all of American territory and history. Yet how relevant to the coming of woman suffrage was that complex of ideas and attitudes encompassed in the concepts of frontier democracy and frontier equalitarianism? There seems to be little evidence that these bold concepts were applied beyond the group of white, adult males; political theorizing seldom reached beyond the confirming conventionalities of race and sex. The rejection of referendums providing for Negro suffrage prior to the passage of the Fifteenth Amendment was paralleled by the rejection of referendums to provide for woman suffrage prior to the passage of the Nineteenth Amendment. While western states were more willing than eastern states to let the male electorate vote on the question of woman suffrage, they also provided greater opportunities in the nineteenth century for rejecting such an extension of the franchise. Kansas in 1867, Michigan in

1874, Colorado in 1877, Nebraska in 1882, Oregon in 1884, Rhode Island in 1887, Washington in 1889, South Dakota in 1890—each had rejected woman suffrage in popular referendums before Colorado became the first state to grant woman suffrage by popular vote in 1893. If we can find in frontier democracy a greater willingness to submit the question to the voters, we must also abide by the typical decision of the electorate that frontier democracy was restricted to men only. Indeed, one finds scant mention of women at all in the robust, masculine prose of that champion of frontier democracy, Turner; for him the frontier provided the setting for a struggle of classic proportions and enduring consequences: the conquest of the virgin land by the indomitable male pioneer.

While grand and simplified theoretical explanations of basic political changes are always tempting, upon close examination, they are often found to be misleading. The frontier equalitarianism explanation for woman suffrage in the West suffers in addition from a confusion of causes and consequences. It argues that along the frontier the forces of Nature were indeed the great equalizer; equalitarian conditions were thereupon proven, so to speak, by such equalitarian political actions as the elimination of property qualifications for voting and, later, the democratic checks on political power best summed up in Populism. Now there is a real question, which will be explored later, whether the equalitarian results in the West were indeed inspired by equalitarian motives or whether they were simply by-products of a struggle for power in which victory rather than equality was the consuming desire. In any case the hypothesis of frontier equalitarianism as an explanation for the coming of woman suffrage in the West is inadequate at the outset, for it never comprehended a political equality for women at all, any more than it included in its scope Negroes, Chinese, Japanese, or in some cases Spanish-Americans.[27] These latter groups were external to the system and not included in the hypothesis. To search further for the factors which contributed to the coming of woman suffrage in the West we must examine the social forces in conflict in the two territories which were the first to adopt woman suffrage, Wyoming and Utah, to see what role such forces played in achieving this equalitarian result.

*

Any inquiry into the social origins of woman suffrage in the West must come to grips with two basic questions: Why the time? Why the place? The first four states to adopt woman suffrage, Wyoming, Colorado, Utah, and Idaho, did so during the last decade of the nineteenth century. Colorado and Idaho achieved woman suffrage through referendums on this issue, the former in 1893, the latter in 1896. Wyoming and Utah, however, had woman suffrage drafted into their state constitutions and they were permitted to retain it at the time of their admission into the Union; the former in 1890, the latter in 1896. Wyoming and Utah were exceptional in still another sense; they were, as territories, the first to adopt woman suffrage by action of their territorial legislatures. Wyoming enacted woman suffrage in December 1869; Utah followed three months later in February 1870. Both of these territories had long experience with woman suffrage: Wyoming, up to statehood some 21 years later; Utah, up to 1887 when Congress abolished woman suffrage there in its effort to destroy polygamy among the Mormons. We may now sharpen the focus of our inquiry to ask why, during the winter of 1869–1870, did the territorial legislatures of Wyoming and Utah enact woman suffrage?

At the outset it should be noted that no two territories could have been more dissimilar than Wyoming and Utah in 1870. Wyoming, wild, boisterous, and unsettled, with a total population of less than 10,000 and at least a 6 to 1 ratio of adult men to adult women, had officially become a territory only in 1868. Utah, the Great Basin Zion of the Church of Latter-day Saints, had been a living political community virtually since the day, in 1847, that Brigham Young had led some 11,000 followers there to found the state of Deseret. Utah was granted territorial status in 1850, and by 1870 had a population of nearly 87,000, approximately evenly distributed by sex. Held together by the common acceptance of a strict, puritanical religious ethic, the theocracy of Utah resembled nothing else in the American experience quite so much as the original Puritan settlement of Massachusetts Bay. Wyoming on the other hand was, for the quarter century prior to its becoming a territory, a land that virtually defied settlement. It was a mountain barrier between the Great Plains and the Pacific slopes, an ordeal to be overcome by the 300,000 pioneers who trekked along the banks of the North Platte, up the Sweetwater and across South Pass to the Green River, or westward still to the Snake River in that remarkable American migration which traveled the Oregon Trail. Many crossed Wyoming; few remained to settle there. What social values could Wyoming and Utah have in common that would cause them to adopt woman suffrage?

The timing of woman suffrage is more easily explained than its location. After the Civil War the question of suffrage for Negroes and for women became a topic of national concern. (Ironically, it was the Fourteenth Amendment which placed the word "male" in the United States Constitution.) In 1869, the two major organizations sponsoring woman suffrage were established to popularize the cause: the National Woman Suffrage Association and the American Woman Suffrage Association. There is no need here to trace the organized activity of these two groups (which merged in 1890) to bring about woman suffrage by either national or state action.[28] It is sufficient to note that these suffrage associations, based essentially in the East, reflected as well as molded an increasing public awareness of the subject. In December 1866, when a bill conferring the franchise on Negroes in the District of Columbia was being debated in the Senate, the issue of woman suffrage was also raised. At that time Senator Henry B. Anthony of Rhode Island noted:

> The discussion of this subject is not confined to visionary enthusiasts. It is now attracting the attention of some of the best thinkers in the world, both in this country and in Europe; and one of the very best of them all, John Stuart Mill, in a most elaborate and able paper, has declared his conviction of the right and justice of female suffrage. The time has not come for it, but the time is coming. It is coming with the progress of civilization and the general amelioration of the race, and the triumph of truth, and justice, and equal rights.

To which, Senator George H. Williams, from the frontier state of Oregon, replied:

> When the women of this country come to be sailors and soldiers; when they come to navigate the ocean and to follow the plow; when they love to be jostled and crowded by all sorts of men in the thoroughfares of trade and business; when they love the treachery and the turmoil of politics; when they love the dissoluteness of the camp, and

the smoke of the thunder, and the blood of battle better than they love the affections and enjoyments of home and family, then it will be time to talk about making the women voters; but, until that time, the question is not fairly before the country.[29]

After the Civil War, when the Fourteenth and Fifteenth Amendments were being discussed and ratified, woman suffrage, while subordinated to the Reconstruction issue of Negro suffrage, could be granted by those states or territories which might wish to adopt it. In most states this adoption could take place only after a constitutional amendment, which in turn required not only legislative endorsement but approval in a referendum as well. In the territories, however, the process was far simpler, usually requiring only an enactment of the territorial legislature with the approval of the territorial governor. There were thus technical advantages to adopting woman suffrage in the territories rather than in the states. In South Dakota, in 1872, the territorial legislature failed by one vote to establish woman suffrage; while in Washington Territory twice (in 1883 and in 1887) the territorial legislature enacted woman suffrage only to have the enactments declared void, on technical grounds, by the territorial supreme court. In Wyoming, however, woman suffrage remained in effect, as doubtless it would have in Utah had Congress not intervened. Why woman suffrage came about in Utah and why Congress intervened to abolish it there will be discussed in the next chapter.

CHAPTER II

The Puritans in Utah

Nothing can be more idle, nothing more frivolous, than to imagine that this polygamy had anything to do with personal licentiousness. If Joseph Smith had proposed to the Latter-day Saints that they should live licentious lives, they would have rushed on him and probably anticipated their pious neighbors who presently shot him.

George Bernard Shaw

In 1870 the legislature of the predominantly Mormon Territory of Utah enacted a statute which granted woman suffrage; in 1887 Congress enacted a statute, the Edmunds-Tucker Act, which abolished woman suffrage in that territory. Although the Territory of Utah had woman suffrage for seventeen years, little attempt was made by the eastern woman suffrage organizations to capitalize on this successful experiment. Indeed, on the eve of the abolition of woman suffrage in Utah, the astute Susan B. Anthony was reported to have said only that the "suffrage is as much of a success for the Mormon women as for the men." [1] To have emphasized the success of woman suffrage in Utah might have implied approval for that other Mormon institution, polygamy; in fact, in Utah, the issues of polygamy and woman suffrage were intertwined.

Because these issues were interrelated, and under the

cognizance of the Mormon Church leadership, there is some mystery surrounding the exact origins of the enactment. There is no evidence of a public discussion having taken place in Utah on woman suffrage prior to its enactment by the territorial legislature, nor indeed of any public discussion on the issue at all until just prior to its overthrow by Congress in 1887. In spite of these handicaps we may reasonably reconstruct the sequence of events by such evidence as does exist and the consensus of scholars who have dealt with the issue.[2] In the course of this reconstruction it will be argued that Mormonism in the nineteenth century, in spite of polygamy, represented the Puritan ethic, and that woman suffrage came about in Utah to bolster the power of the Mormon Church in its effort to defend that ethic.

*

To understand the social values which gave rise to woman suffrage in Utah it is important to see in the social doctrines of the Church of Latter-day Saints a renaissance of the Puritan ethic of piety, sobriety, industry, frugality, and asceticism. "The same religious stock," *Tullidge's Quarterly Magazine* observed in 1881, "which in the Seventeenth Century formed the Cromwellian Puritans, in the Eighteenth Century became Wesleyan Methodists, and, in the Nineteenth Century, Mormons."[3] Leonard J. Arrington, in his comprehensive economic history of the Mormons, *Great Basin Kingdom*, reports further:

> Mormonism . . . had a particularly strong appeal to the descendents of the New England Puritans. Its comprehensive theology, Old Testament literalism, militant faith, and providential interpretation of history, coupled with the "chosen people of God" concept, attracted particu-

larly the sons and daughters of New England who were discontented with the theology and polity of contemporary Calvinism. The closeness of the Mormons to their fatherly God, His believed interest in their daily affairs, and the direct and complete influence of church over their spiritual and temporal lives indicate a considerable and significant reaction against contemporary Calvinist absolutism and deistic secularism. Most of the early members, and virtually all of the early leaders who shaped the faith, including Brigham Young, were born in New England or were of New England parentage.[4]

It is not sympathetic critics alone who have found a relationship of Mormonism to Puritanism; hostile critics in the nineteenth century sometimes dwelt upon this relationship for adverse comment. For example, a writer in *Harper's Magazine* in 1881 observed that "the mixed Puritanism and Mohammedanism in the soul of [John] Smith, which gave origin and direction to the Mormon institution, still control the spirit of affairs in Utah. By Puritanism we mean, above, that kind that burned witches, and compelled men to worship God in one way. It is but a little while ago, in a village but a few miles from Salt Lake City, that a woman was shot for being a 'witch' " [5]

Like their Puritan predecessors in New England, the Mormons were remarkable community builders. As a Mormon petition to Congress in 1870 observed, they "reclaimed the desert waste, cultivated it, subdued the Indians, opened means of communication, made roads, built cities, towns, and settlements, established government, encouraged education. . . ." [6] And like the migration of their Puritan ancestors coming to the New World or following Thomas Hooker into Connecticut or Roger Williams into Rhode Island, the Mormon migration was a family movement. From Maine, Vermont, upper New York, Pennsylvania, Ohio, and, later, from England and the Scandinavian countries, husbands and wives, sons and daughters streamed into the Great Basin of Utah in family groups and caravans of families. In this they were unlike other migrations to the western frontier, in which young men did the advance scouting and returned later with their families. Typically the fringes of settlement contained a highly disproportionate ratio of men to women, but in Utah the family pattern of migration kept the balance between the sexes essentially equal.

The Mormon migration was remarkable in still another sense: the way was always prepared for these settlers, with posts of supplies and provisions along the route, with directions for settlement and arrangements for employment upon arrival. Whether due to the experience of hardship and privation of previous migrations—from New York to Ohio, to Missouri, to Illinois, to Utah—or the extraordinary organizing genius and leadership of Brigham Young and the upper hierarchy of the church, or the invincible dedication and determination of a people fully convinced they were chosen by God to fulfill their mission, the Mormon settlement of Utah was probably the most successful experiment in large-scale social planning and social engineering in American history. This ambitious experiment in community building, however, was made easier by the fact that generations did not have to pass before a sense of community developed; the family settlers brought it with them. They came to Utah, remote, inaccessible and still largely unknown, because they already possessed the essential ingredient of any community, a common sense of identity, which they brought with them to the Great Basin. As a self-perceived "chosen people"—they termed those not of

the faith "gentiles"—they possessed a community of outlook, of interest, of style of life.

Inevitably, in such a community the affairs of man in
this world, whether of an economic, political, social or religious nature, were of vital concern to the church leadership, which saw itself charged with the awesome responsibility of maintaining the ways of the Lord among His
chosen people. By the time of the Civil War, this temporal
Zion had all but developed a self-sufficient economy based
upon farming, grazing, and such manufacturing as was
needed for use within the territory. This essentially self-
contained system might fear only two conceivable threats
to its security: intervention by the federal government or a
great influx of gentiles hostile to Mormonism.

The first threat, federal intervention, was the greater: in
the Republican platform of 1856, the Mormon practice of
polygamy had been declared, along with slavery, one of the
"twin relics of barbarism," which required extermination.
Mormon Puritanism, because it included polygamy, an-
tagonized other faiths by arousing prejudices that were far
older than Puritanism itself. Eventually, monogamist morality was considerably offended to learn that Brigham
Young had 27 wives and 56 children.[7] In vain did the
Mormon leaders point to the Old Testament acceptance of
polygamy as a legitimate social institution, to the practical
reasonableness of polygamy in a society in which women
tended to survive men, to the advantages of polygamy to
women themselves, for none need be an old maid and lose
the opportunity to have children. One defender of polygamy wrote:

> Shall such virtuous and innocent females, though they
> may be poor and low in the scale of fortune's partial
> smiles—shall they be denied the right to choose the ob-

jects of their love? Must they . . . be virtually doomed to resort to infamous prostitution, entailing disease, infamy, and death upon themselves and their off-spring, or to marry an inferior race of corrupt, vicious men . . . or remain in perpetual celibacy and frustrate the designs of their creation . . . to multiply and replenish the earth? [8]

Professor Arrington argues that in the great and long sustained opposition to Mormonism the fundamental issues "were not so much a matter of plural marriage and other reprehensible peculiarities and superstitions as of the conflicting economic patterns of two generations of Americans, one of which was fashioned after the communitarian concepts of the age of Jackson, and the other of which was shaped by the dream of bonanza and the individualistic sentiments of the age of laissez-faire." [9] However, whatever economic forces might have lurked in the background awaiting an opportunity to break up the Mormon economic and political monopoly in the Great Basin, there seems ample evidence that polygamy was what most of the critics were writing about and talking about. It was this issue which brought Harriet Beecher Stowe into the ranks of the Mormon opposition. "May we not then hope," Mrs. Stowe declared, "that the hour is come to loose the bonds of cruel slavery whose chains have cut into the very hearts of thousands of our sisters—a slavery which debases and degrades womanhood, motherhood, and the family?" [10] At bottom there would seem to have been two systems of conscience in conflict, one polygamous, the other monogamous; each claimed to be the ethically superior system. Kimball Young, a grandson of Brigham Young, summed up the matter neatly in *Isn't One Wife Enough?:*

After the Civil War when the first relic of barbarism had been liquidated, Mormonism and polygamy rivaled with prostitution and prohibition as the main interest of American reformers. Polygamy was a menace to everything which puritanic Americans held sacred. Plural wifehood was an attack upon monogamy, the home and fireside, upon children, and—above all—upon the rising status of women. It was, therefore, the moral duty of all good Christians to help uproot this evil.[11]

To the Mormons, however, there could be no better way of proving that their system of polygamy was not degrading to women, that Mormon wives were not kept in a form of slavery, than to declare woman suffrage in Utah, at the very time when Negro suffrage (by the adoption of the Fifteenth Amendment) was being offered to the former slaves to protect them from their former masters. Although there seems to be no evidence of any public discussion of woman suffrage in Utah at this time, its adoption on February 12, 1870, by the territorial legislature would appear to have been a calculated move on the part of the Mormon hierarchy to forestall federal legislation on polygamy.

The year 1869 was a momentous one in Mormon history. It marked the completion of the transcontinental railroad, and it saw the introduction of the first comprehensive antipolygamy legislation in Congress, by Representative Shelby M. Cullom of Illinois. Indeed, it was during the week that the Cullom bill appeared on the floor of the House for discussion that woman suffrage was enacted in Utah. It was apparently in the fall of 1869 that Brigham Young, and according to a sympathetic account, "far-seeing Mormon leaders," conceived of the woman suffrage bill for the territory.[12] A hostile account has it that at this time "The wily deceiver then evolved from his narrow soul the magnanimous scheme of *enfranchising the women*. The

Mormon legislature passed the bill. The Gentile miners were mostly unmarried men, or had left their families in the East. Every Mormon citizen thus had his civil power extended in correspondence with his numerous alliances." Furthermore, according to this account, "Nearly every member of this Territorial or 'State' legislature was a Mormon high-priest, and was the possessor of from two to seven wives." [13] By all accounts, woman suffrage was brought about by the Mormon Church to serve its own advantage in its struggle to maintain its power in Utah.

Increasingly, by 1870, the power of the Mormon Church was challenged by Congress. William H. Hooper, the territorial delegate from Utah, protested in vain that it was "the unanimous testimony of all that, aside from what they consider the objectionable practice of polygamy, my constituents are sober, moral, just, and industrious in the eyes of all impartial witnesses."

> In this community, removed by long reaches of wastes from the moral influences of civilization, we have a quiet, orderly, and Christian community. Our towns are without gambling-hells, drinking-saloons, or brothels, while from end to end of our territory the innocent can walk unharmed at all hours. Nor is this due to an organized police, but to the kind natures and Christian impulses of a good people. In support of my argument of their entire sincerity I with confidence appeal to their history.[14]

On March 23, 1870, the Cullom bill passed the House by the overwhelming vote of 94 to 32; the Senate failed to act on it. However, it was the harbinger of congressional legislation against polygamy, which culminated in the Edmunds-Tucker Act of 1887.

In addition to hostile congressional legislation the Mormons feared an influx of gentiles who might vote against the system. These votes might be counteracted by the adoption of woman suffrage. It was this threat of gentile voters which became of great consequence after the completion of the railroad in 1869. "Railroads are great civilizers," wrote one anti-Mormon observer. "The snort of the engine is the bugle note of progress." With the coming of the railroad, "The pulse of national life began to be felt in Zion." [15]

It had been the unhappy experience of the Puritans in Massachusetts Bay that, in time, there had been a falling away from the faith and an undermining of control of the established oligarchy, due largely to the influx of non-Puritan immigrants; it had been equally the unhappy experience of the Roman Catholic Church in colonial Maryland that, in time, Protestant immigration led to a Protestant majority which proscribed the practice of Catholicism until after the Revolution. A sustained influx of non-Mormons into Utah was thus realistically seen as a threat to the system. As long as the Great Basin remained essentially isolated from the rest of the country, as long as there were no great material rewards to be obtained in return for the hazards and inconveniences of penetrating this tightly knit religious-socio-economic system, the Mormons could feel reasonable secure. Should this isolation be destroyed, the consequences for the established system would be grave indeed. One writer expressed this belief: "For rolling back the tide of Anglo-American civilization, whenever the tide shall wash over the mountain bounds of Utah, Brother Brigham's bands will be just as efficient as old Mrs. Partington's mop in keeping the Atlantic Ocean out of her back kitchen. . . . When the United States goes to Utah, Mormonism will disappear like a puddle with Niagara Falls turned into it." [16]

Initially it was the miners, the "forty-niners" and "fifty-niners," in California and neighboring Nevada, Colorado, and Wyoming, who posed this threat to the establishment. In Colorado, for example, in five months in 1859 some 100,000 miners swarmed over the mountains after the strike at Gregory Gulch.[17] Such an overpowering influx into Utah might well have spelled disaster to the Mormon establishment. By various means, which need not be noted here, Mormon leaders attempted to discourage the immigration of gentile miners. In an article entitled, "The Mormons and Mining," in the Salt Lake *Herald* (September 18, 1887) this general attitude was summed up:

> If Mormons have seemed to oppose the development of mines by Gentiles, it is because they have realized the probability of the influx of a great population, which, through the influence of lying priests and politicans, might seek to re-enact the scenes of Missouri and Kansas. If there were some competent power to make a treaty for the Gentile population, which would be honored, and if it were stipulated that the Mormons would receive fair and honest treatment forever at their hands, the latter would not raise a voice in opposition to their coming.[18]

It was, however, unrealistic to expect that the contagion of "gold fever"—next to the Civil War itself the most common topic of discussion in the West—would not spread ultimately into Utah. Nor were there lacking enterprising souls willing to risk the wrath of the Mormons for the chance of obtaining great riches. Such a one was Colonel Patrick E. Connor who, in the fall of 1862, led the California Volunteers into Utah to protect the Overland Mail which ran from Los Angeles to Salt Lake City. In 1863 Connor came across a vein of gold and he thereafter tried to capitalize on his findings, an operation fraught with economic difficulties until the railroads could provide a more satisfactory system of transportation. Clearly, Connor had a financial interest which put him in conflict with the Mormons, but, judging from the tone of his correspondence, he had a dislike of the Mormons which must have gone much deeper than the pocketbook. On one occasion, for example, he wrote to the Assistant Adjutant General in San Francisco:

> My policy in this territory has been to invite hither a large Gentile and loyal population, sufficient by peaceful means and through the ballot box to overwhelm the Mormons by mere force of numbers, and thus wrest from the church—disloyal and traitorous to the core—the absolute and tyrannical control of temporal and civil affairs, or at least a population numerous enough to put a check on the Mormon authorities, and give countenance to those who are striving to loosen the bonds with which they have been so long oppressed. With this view I have bent every energy and means of which I was possessed, both personal and official, towards the discovery of mining resources of the territory, using without stint the soldiers of my command, whenever and wherever it could be done without detriment to the public service.[19]

It should be evident, however, that with a reserve force of Mormon women voters on tap, Colonel Connor's importation of gentile miners at least for a time presented no threat.

It has been argued here that the enactment of woman suffrage by the Mormon-controlled territorial legislature of Utah in 1870 was a politically inspired move to protect the Church against congressional anti-polygamy legislation, and an influx of gentile settlers borne by the railroads. This view may be further supported not only by the one-sided election statistics during the seventeen years in which women voted—in 1872, for example, the Mormon-drafted constitution for the State of Deseret was approved by a vote of 25,324 for to 368 opposed—but also by the testimony of observers of the politics of Utah.[20]

The Utah statute enacting woman suffrage was a remarkably ambiguous bit of legislation. It read:

> Every woman of the age of twenty-one years, who has resided in this territory six months next preceding any general or special election, born or naturalized in the United States, or who is the wife, widow, or the daughter of a native-born or naturalized citizen of the United States, shall be entitled to vote at any election in this Territory.[21]

As one critic observed, "No qualifications are defined for the female voter, except such as are overruled by the disjunctive 'or'—'or who is the wife, widow, or daughter of a native-born or naturalized citizen.' . . . The woman or girl who is not the wife, widow, or daughter of somebody might justly be denominated 'anomalous.' "[22] It was maintained by the critics of the Mormons that the leniency and breadth of the statute was an intentional part of the strategy to bolster Mormon power, for the suffrage provisions were stricter for men. Native-born male citizens had to be twenty-one years of age, taxpayers, and have residence in the territory for at least six months; naturalized male citizens had not only to have these requirements, but had to have in addition five years' residence in the country.

As a consequence of these suffrage provisions, it was possible for the wives, widows, and daughters of naturalized citizens who were unable to meet the suffrage requirements themselves to be possessed of the ballot. It was evidently assumed that a woman's vote in Utah was a Mormon vote. According to one critic of woman suffrage in Utah: "Under that law girls under age, and alien women with the odor of the emigrant ship still upon their clothes, without even having taken an oath of allegiance to the United States, without the slightest idea of the meaning of the acts they are performing, or what is intended by it, cast their votes as they are instructed to, in some tongue unknown to ordinary Americans, and go away dazed." [23] A Mrs. Fanny Stenhouse reported of woman suffrage in Utah: "I have often seen one solitary man driving into the city a whole wagon load of women of all ages and sizes. They were going to the polls and their vote would be one." [24] A Bishop Lunt, of the Mormon Church, was reported by the *San Francisco Chronicle* to have said: "Our vote is solid and will always remain so. It will be thrown where the most good will be accomplished for the church. The women of Utah vote, and they never desert the colors of the church; they vote for the tried friends of the church. You can imagine the results which wisdom may bring about, with the assistance of a church organization like ours." [25] It was suggested by some that woman suffrage applied as well to gentile as to Mormon women. Critics responded, however, with the observation that "The centers of Gentile representation are the mining districts. Most of the miners are unmarried men, or men who have left their families in the East. The vote of the Mormon women nullifies Gentile political power in these districts." [26]

All available evidence supports the conclusion that Mormon women voted in support of the Mormon establishment. In March 1886, when Congress was considering legislation to abolish woman suffrage in Utah because it supported the Mormon Church, some 2000 Mormon women gathered in Salt Lake City to protest such federal legislation and to memorialize Congress with the following: *"Resolved by the women of Utah in mass meeting assembled,* That the suffrage originally conferred upon us as a political privilege has become a vested right by possession and usage for fifteen years, and that we *protest* against being deprived of that right without process of law, and for no other reason than that we do not vote to suit our political opponents."²⁷ Clearly, the Mormon women revealed that they voted as one, to the annoyance of the anti-Mormons.

*

What emerges in a study of the origins of woman suffrage in Utah Territory is the absence of any trace of equality of the sexes in the issue. There is no reason to derive such equality from the doctrine of the Church of Latter-day Saints; indeed, there is every reason to derive the typically nineteenth-century assumptions of masculine superiority from both church doctrine and established practices. Generalizations about frontier equalitarianism, furthermore, are simply not relevant to the situation in Utah in 1870, for the Mormons had established in the Great Basin what were surely the most civilized communities found in any of the territories of that time.

Like the early Puritans of Massachusetts Bay, the Mormons of Utah placed a high premium on a strictly enforced set of values for the community, values which comprehended at one time theology, economics, and politics. These values regulated personal behavior as much as they did public policy. A sense of mission, a feeling of divine calling, permeates much of the Mormon literature on the building of their Zion. "In some respects," the Mormon historian Andrew Love Neff once wrote, "it seemed that Brigham Young had picked up the thread of life where Jonathan Edwards and Cotton Mather laid it down." [28] Or, as a recent writer has observed: "The Mormon faith, like the Puritan, had developed its principles and grown in a land which could no longer hold them. Both were built on the assumption that the church was divine and eternal, that they were under divine auspices; both needed isolation to develop; and both established theocratic government in a wilderness." [29] With the coming of the railroad, however, the isolation was destroyed and the polygamist theocracy was confronted with the typical attitudes on marriage and church and state relations of the rest of the United States. The new Puritanism of Utah found itself in conflict with a society which had long since departed, in many respects, from the rigid doctrine and style of life of the older Puritanism.

The issue of woman suffrage in Utah territory was clearly bound up with the coming of the railroad, with polygamy, with the gentile search for wealth and the Mormon search for ways to preserve their church and its domain. What eventuated was an undisguised struggle for power between the church hierarchy and the national government, between the Mormons and their supporters, and the anti-Mormons and theirs. Women voters were not so much pawns in this struggle as reserve troops to be called upon when needed. To see only the quasi-equalitarian result (woman suffrage) of this struggle without focusing on the factors and forces which led up to it is to miss the essential meaning of the conflict. For the conflict was not one involving equalitarianism, or some form of woman's rights, but the hegemony of the system of values and the structure of power in the Territory of Utah. The nearest parallel to the conflict was of course the recent one of the Civil War itself—not because the Mormon women in any sense were in bondage tantamount to slavery, as the anti-Mormons charged—but because a small sectional style of life was in conflict with a national norm: a communitarian, co-operative economic system was challenged by an exploitative, capitalistic one; an almost ascetic norm of personal and social behavior, which disdained the use of stimulants—coffee, tea, tobacco, and liquor—censured promiscuity and gambling, and practiced tithing to support the church, was countered by a lusty, individualistic response which rejected the Mormon conception of vice as narrow, unrealistic, and inhibiting, and saw in indulgence the solace of loneliness, the reward for fatigue, and the spoils of the successful.

That these opposing styles of life produced some observable social consequences is, in part, attested to by the historian Hubert Howe Bancroft, who compiled some statistics on the incidence of crime during the years 1880–82. Of some 1786 crimes reported in Utah and in Mormon communities in neighboring Idaho, only 208 were committed by Mormons. In the major categories of murder, manslaughter, and rape, no Mormons were involved, though 10 non-Mormons were; 62 non-Mormons committed robbery and burglary, but only 4 Mormons; 174 non-Mormons were convicted of prostitution, brothel keeping, and gambling, but no members of the Church of Latter-day Saints. Some 109 Mormons were found guilty of drunkenness, compared to 594 non-Mormons. No Mormons were convicted of vagrancy, but 174 non-Mormons were.[30] Still later, in 1889, a non-Mormon Utah Commissioner, A. B. Carlton, reported:

> I was not long in discovering that one was as safe in Salt Lake City by day or night as in any other city of the United States. . . . Later I ascertained that if a man should be sandbagged, robbed, or have his home burglarized, the chances were ten to one that the perpetrator would be an "outsider" and not a "Mormon." It is a fact, shown by statistics, that while only about one-fifth of the population are Gentiles, they contribute at least four-fifths of the crimes of a heinous character. The same proportions will hold good as to the misdemeanors— excepting, of course, polygamy.[31]

Prior to the coming of the railroad, there were no political parties in Utah; where nearly all were in agreement of the fundamental articles of faith, and theology and politics were interrelated, the consensus in religion seemed to preclude political division. In July 1870, the first secular political party in Utah, the gentile Liberal party, was established in Corinne, with Patrick E. Connor elected chairman of its first convention. It proclaimed a platform which opposed polygamy, opposed the union of church and state, and encouraged mining in the territory. It also nominated General George R. Maxwell as the territorial delegate for Congress. The Mormon hierarchy responded with the People's party which included in its ranks the newly enfranchised woman voters.[32] A one-sided contest resulted, with the Liberal party candidate receiving fewer than 1500 votes (of which some half were alleged to be fraudulent) out of a total of over 20,000. The Liberal party, however, posed no real threat to the Mormon hierarchy as long as Mormon women voted. In 1880, a decade after the coming of competitive party politics to Utah, the balance of power

remained essentially what it had been in 1870: the delegate to Congress of the People's party (Mormon) received
16,668 votes; the Liberal party (gentile) candidate,
1357.[33] In 1886, the last election for territorial delegate
to Congress in which women voters were eligible, the Liberal party candidate received less than 3000 out of a total
of approximately 20,000 votes, after some 12,000 Mormons
had been disfranchised, under the Edmunds Act of 1882,
for supporting polygamy.

There is no need here to review the congressional legislation and federal court cases which led to the breakdown
of the Mormon system and the abandonment of polygamy
as an article of faith. It is enough to note that, in March
1887, Congress passed the Edmunds-Tucker Act, directed
at breaking up the Mormon system in Utah. It contained,
among its many prohibitory features, a provision which
abolished woman suffrage in the territory. Thus, the only
federal legislation on woman suffrage in the nineteenth
century was an Act which abolished it in Utah. Once
again, equalitarianism had nothing to do with the issue,
which involved only the problem of political and—to a
lesser degree—economic power in the Mormon territory.
One student has estimated that, while the abolition of
woman suffrage scarcely affected the gentile voting
strength, it cut the Mormon vote in half.[34] In any event,
commencing in 1887, the Liberal party was able to elect a
few members to the territorial legislature, although it still
could not elect a delegate to Congress. In 1889, the Liberal
party gained control of both Salt Lake City and Ogden;
clearly, the struggle for power was coming to a climax. It
was reached the following year. In 1890, in the space of a
few months three notable decisions took place: in May, the
U. S. Supreme Court upheld the congressional legislation

and subsequent executive action which in effect took control of the property of the Mormon Church (in the *Late Corporation of the Church of Jesus Christ of Latter-day Saints* v. *the United States* (136 US 1); in June, the People's party disbanded; in September, Wilford Woodruff, as president of the church, issued the "Mormon Manifesto" ending polygamy as an article of faith.

> In as much as laws have been enacted by Congress forbidding plural marriage, I hereby declare my intention to submit to those laws, and to use my influence with the members of the Church over which I preside to have them do likewise. . . . And I now publicly declare that my advice to the Latter-day Saints is to refrain from contracting any marriage forbidden by the law of the land.[35]

In the election of 1892, national political parties functioned for the first time in Utah. In 1894, when Utah elected delegates to a convention to draft a state constitution, both parties pledged themselves to woman suffrage. It has been reported that by this time, "Of her people, 8 out of 10 were American-born and nearly 9 out of 10 were Latter-day Saints." [36] The endorsement of woman suffrage by both parties would seem to indicate that, once the power of the Mormon Church had been checked, the issue of woman suffrage was no longer a major issue of political disagreement. Yet, even so, the woman suffrage provision in the new constitution was the most discussed item at the convention. Of the 107 elected delegates to the convention, some 28 were non-Mormons. The anti-woman suffrage side was led by Mormon Democrat Brigham H. Roberts, who feared Congress might reject Utah's application for statehood if woman suffrage were restored. When the issue came to a vote, however, the woman suffrage forces won handily enough, 75 to 14.[37] The woman suffrage side clearly drew support from Mormons and gentiles alike, as it did from both Republicans and Democrats. In 1896 the state of Utah was admitted into the Union with woman suffrage in its constitution.

We may now generalize on at least the evidence drawn from the limited experience of Utah with woman suffrage: woman suffrage came about in the Territory of Utah not because there was more democracy or equalitarianism in the Mormon Kingdom than elsewhere, but because woman suffrage was a politically expedient and efficacious method of bolstering the voting strength, social values, and organizational structure of the regime in power; woman suffrage was intended to, and did, support the *status quo*. In spite of polygamy the Mormon social outlook may be best described by the term Puritan; it was in effect these Puritan values which woman suffrage was called upon to defend. Conversely, woman suffrage was prohibited in Utah in an effort to upset the structure of power and system of values of the Mormons. As part of a comprehensive congressional attack upon the Mormon regime, the denial of woman suffrage was clearly an effective action. What must now be explored is the situation in neighboring Wyoming, a non-Mormon territory, to see whether any useful generalizations might be made which would comprehend the issue of woman suffrage in these two quite dissimilar territories.

CHAPTER III

The Civilizers of Wyoming

The vote of women transformed Wyoming from
barbarism to civilization.

National Woman Suffrage Association, 1880

In Utah, woman suffrage constituted part of a broad effort
to retain a civilization; in Wyoming, woman suffrage was a
major factor in establishing one. Woman suffrage in Wyoming
was in a sense a product of the frontier; it represented
a reaction to it. It was, so to speak, the other side of
the frontier, the side which Louis B. Wright wrote about
in his perceptive *Culture on the Moving Frontier*:

> The anarchistic and disintegrating forces of the frontier
> met another force less violent but eternally steady in its
> pressure. The determination of a few persistent men and
> women to re-create in the wilderness a stable social order
> with its traditional amenities. This conflict between anarchy
> and civilization was not spectacular; its battles were
> not often sufficiently dramatic to become the theme of
> ballad, novel, or movie. But the struggle was clearly defined
> and men could see what was happening.[1]

In order to see this issue properly, it is well to consider it
against the background conditions: the vastness of the terrain,
the sparseness of the population, the fluidity of the
social structure, and the instability and uncertainty of gov-

ernment in the formative days of the territory. The immensity of Wyoming provided at the outset an enormous problem of government. Over twice the size of New York —all six New England states, plus New York and New Jersey could fit inside Wyoming—it had a population in 1869 of only 8014 people, or the equivalent of about one person per twelve square miles. Into this vast terrain, and usually through it, streamed a continuing influx of transients. Early Wyoming history is a record of trails and transportation, of a territory to be conquered and crossed under the watchful presence of the Indians; of the Oregon Trail, of the Mormon passage into Utah, of the Central, Overland, California and Pike's Peak Express Company, and of that costly, romantic but short-lived endeavor, the Pony Express. To Wyoming, as to Utah, the turning point in history came with the establishment of the transcontinental railroad.

In the years 1867–68 some 10,000 men worked their way across Wyoming laying down track for the railroad. The initial impact of the railroad on Wyoming, however, was found in the kinds of people it brought in.

"Hell on Wheels" was the contemporary name given to the transient community which spearheaded the course of railroad construction. Wyoming had been a part of the Dakota Territory at the time that the railroad was begun. Apparently, the realization that this potentially troublesome, transient railroading population outnumbered the rest of the Dakota residents caused the settled Dakotans to favor a slicing off of the railroad portion of the territory. The Territory of Wyoming was thus established in 1868 by Congress out of parts of Dakota, Utah, and Idaho, at the very time the railway line was completing its transit of the area.[2]

In July of 1867, the advance camp of the railroad, the "Hell on Wheels," reached what is now Cheyenne, the first railroad terminus in Wyoming; the town was incorporated by the Dakota legislature later that year. Some conception of what Cheyenne must have been like just two years prior to the enactment of woman suffrage may be seen in the following historical description:

By November, 1867, Cheyenne population had reached 4,000, and lots that sold originally for $150 were bringing speculators $2,500. Citizens lived in anything that would shed rain and sun: covered wagon boxes, dugouts, tents, shacks. More than 3,000 such dwellings had been erected within six months. . . .

Commentators invariably associated the terminal town with Hell, and Cheyenne's reputation ranked with that of Julesburg. General Dodge said in 1868 that it was the gambling center of the world, and its reputation grew with its population. . . .

The seditious nature of the frontier is generally overdrawn, but Cheyenne inherited all the lawlessness of the Hell-on-Wheels, in addition to its own soldiery and flotsam. Liquor was cheap, pay was good, and stakes were high for gamblers, confidence men, promoters, and robbers. Soldiers and workers alike were just out of a four-year war where they had been schooled at length in the strategy of quick decision and action. Deaths were frequent, often violent; the cemetery was as essential as the post office. Both came second to the saloon. Enraged Indians and white ruffians were not the worker's only potential enemies. A drunken friend or straying bullets from someone else's quarrel could be as dangerous. Many workers became as callous and excitable as the bad folk. "Hell must have been raked to furnish them," one early Cheyenne visitor said, "and to Hell must they naturally return after graduating here." [3]

To this rather grim description of the elements which made up Cheyenne in its beginnings may be added that of an early resident, Malcolm Campbell, who recalled:

> There were tents set everywhere without alignment, and the scaffoldings of new buildings were being erected to the tune of many hammers, the lumber having been hauled all the way from Denver. There were tents where men sat on benches before long plank tables wolfing meals; tents with rough shelves of canned goods piled to the eaves, and many others where sat gamblers playing faro, roulette and monte.
>
> Saloons were everywhere with their bourbons, whiskeys, brandies and beers. Hurdy-gurdies could be heard in any block at any time of the day or night. Along the banks of Crow Creek were grouped the canvas-covered wagons of emigrants. Camp fires blazed continuously and shelters had been erected on ropes stretched from wheel to wheel.
>
> The aisles between the tents in the town were swarming with the roughest of the population. Idlers sauntered from gambling table to dance hall, then on to saloon. Others stood in groups debating the probable boom in real estate values within the next few days. Water wells were being dug at four of the corners of what was to be a business block. Everywhere was expectancy and alertness.
>
> As in the case of all new towns, the gamblers, thieves and so-called sporting elements were running things with a high hand. I heard that it was a nightly occurence for men to be knocked on the head, dragged off into the dark and robbed of all possessions. Everyone wore guns, minded his own business and demanded that other men mind theirs.[4]

In the spring of 1868, the railroad moved on to Laramie, leaving behind in Cheyenne a population of approximately 1500, a demoralized provisional government, and a grimly effective vigilance committee. As the "Hell on Wheels" progressed westward across Wyoming, the pattern of chaos and lawlessness established in Cheyenne advanced with it. In April 1868, the railroad sold lots in the recently charted townsite of Laramie.

Within a week 400 plots had been sold at prices ranging from $25 to $260. Ten days later 500 shacks had been erected of logs, canvas, condemned railroad ties, and dismantled wagon boxes. The first train slid down the steep grade into town on May 9, 1868, and with the train came all the population and paraphernalia of "Hell-on-Wheels." The first freight carried iron rails, crossties, plows, scrapers, tents, portable shanties, lumber, groceries, cookstoves, crockery, tinware, liquors, and the transient population of the terminal town: gamblers, workers, harlots, hunters, migratory shop and saloon-keepers, peddlers with their packs, and straggling settlers' families.[5]

It was against this background of lawlessness and chaos, aggravated by the presence of a proportionately large transient population, that organized government and woman suffrage were established in Wyoming. In Utah, by way of contrast, the politically organized community of Saints had long prepared for the chaos expected to accompany the coming of the railroad. Furthermore, in Utah the railroad skirted the periphery of the Mormon settlements. When the lines connecting the Mormon cities and towns were laid, they were built largely by Mormon labor under the direction of Mormon supervisors. In Wyoming, however, the railroad came before the establishment of effective organized government in that territory; thus the chaos the railroad brought added to the unstable situation already existing. And the very location of the railroad further contributed to the disorder. Because of the mountainous terrain, the railroad track had to be laid along the valleys and passes that made up the most accessible and convenient route to the west. In Utah the railroads all but by-passed the established communities, but in Wyoming the railroads virtually determined the location of future communities. Cheyenne, Laramie, South Pass emerged as cities in the wake of the railroad. In Utah there was a unifying ethic of common religious faith which had originally brought about the settlements and which served as a normative guide to behavior in the face of an influx of outsiders. In Wyoming there was no unifying system of belief or code of behavior; Wyoming approximated a Hobbesian state of nature, with one's life in continual jeopardy.

In May 1868, a provisional government was established in Laramie; by summer, lawlessness was rampant and chaos reigned; by fall, a vigilante force of some five hundred men had been established in an attempt to bring order to the community. Laramie, which had been established under the jurisdiction of the Dakota territorial legislature, now had its charter revoked by that body, and the town was placed under the jurisdiction of the federal courts, where it remained until 1874, five years after the organization of Wyoming as a territory. It was during this period of Laramie's history that Laramie women first sat on grand and petit juries.

On May 10, 1869, the transcontinental railroad was officially completed. A census taken a few months later of Wyoming Territory showed a population of 2665 in Laramie County (which included Cheyenne), 2027 in Albany County (which included Laramie), and 3322 in the remainder of the territory.[6] With a total population just exceeding 8000, there were less than 2000 females in the territory, or a male-female ratio of at least 3 to 1. Among adults, however, the male-female ratio was nearly 6 to 1. In contrast to Utah, where family migration prevailed and the distribution of the sexes remained basically even, in Wyoming the normal pattern of migration throughout the Rocky Mountain region existed: first came the men; later came the women and their families. By 1880, when the population of Wyoming had increased to nearly 21,000, there were still only about 3200 women of voting age in the territory. At best, the coming of woman suffrage in 1869 affected only a few hundred families; undoubtedly, however, it doubled the potential vote of the resident married householder.

*

In newly emerging societies, decidedly significant political actions may be the result largely of pure chance, coincidence, or a fortuitous combination of circumstances. In old societies with established political systems, public policy must follow in some measure along the well-worn paths of custom and tradition, ever mindful of the need for sustaining a consensus. The granting of woman suffrage in Wyoming in 1869 by enactment of the first territorial legislature was in large measure the product of chance and circumstance, bearing only the most tenuous relationship to the eastern woman suffrage movement of the day. In the *History of Woman Suffrage,* J. W. Kingman, associate justice of the supreme court of Wyoming Territory noted:

> It is evident that there was no public sentiment demanding the passage of the woman suffrage law, and but few advocates of it at that time in the territory; that its adoption, under such circumstances, was not calculated to

give it a fair chance to exert a favorable influence in the community, or even maintain itself among the permanent customs and laws of the territory.[7]

The first territorial election, in September 1869, was by all accounts a boisterous, chaotic, and probably fraudulent affair in which the numerous frontier-town saloons played a major role in assisting prospective voters in their political decisions. Indeed, a total of 5264 votes was recorded as having been cast for the delegate to Congress in 1869, when the census figures for the territory totaled only 8014; the number of votes was quite out of line with subsequent election statistics.[8]

In the first territorial legislature, all nine elected members of the council were Democrats, as were all twelve of the representatives in the House. The governor, John A. Campbell, a Grant appointee, was Republican. The woman suffrage bill was introduced by Council President W. H. Bright of Carter county (South Pass City, a gold mining town) on November 27, 1869. It passed the council on November 30, by a vote of 6 ayes, 2 nays, 1 absent. On December 6, the bill passed the House by a vote of 7 ayes and 4 nays. It was signed by Governor Campbell on December 10, 1869. Thus it was enacted:

That every woman of the age of twenty-one years residing in this Territory may at every election to be holden under the laws thereof cast her vote; and her rights to the elective Franchise, and to hold office, shall be the same under the election laws of the Territory as those of electors.[9]

Accounts vary as to just what motivated Councilman Bright to initiate his notable proposal, or why indeed it should have been approved by that legislature. The same legislature also passed a bill protecting the right of married women to hold separate property, as well as a bill prohibiting pay discrimination against women teachers. Yet before one proceeds too far with assumptions of frontier equalitarianism, it should be noted that this legislature also enacted legislation prohibiting intermarriage of whites and Negroes.

Dr. Anna Howard Shaw, a stanch suffragette, suggests in *Story of a Pioneer* that Councilman Bright was indebted to a Mrs. Esther Morris, of South Pass City, for her assistance during his wife's childbirth and repaid his debt by initiating this legislation which Mrs. Morris, favored.[10] A variation of the same account tells how Mrs. Morris, who had recently heard Susan B. Anthony speak in Illinois, invited Bright and other candidates to her house and presented them with a convincing case for woman suffrage.[11] According to Justice Kingman's version, Councilman Bright did his wife's bidding. "His character was not above reproach, but he had an excellent, well-informed wife, and he was a kind, indulgent husband. In fact, he venerated his wife, and submitted to her judgment and influence more willingly than one could have supposed; and she was in favor of woman suffrage." [12] In another variation, Governor Hoyt (governor of Wyoming Territory 1878–82) has Councilman Bright speak to his wife as follows:

"Betty, it's a shame that I should be a member of the legislature and make laws for such a woman as you. You are a great deal better than I am; you know a great deal more, and you would make a better member of the Assembly than I, and you know it. I have been thinking about it and have made up my mind that I will go to work and do everything in my power to give you the ballot. Then you may work out the rest in your own way." [13]

And in a recent study of woman suffrage it is noted that Bright "supported woman suffrage because the ballot had just been given to the Negro, and it galled him to keep it from his wife." [14]

Whatever may have been the interesting motives which led Councilman Bright to introduce the woman suffrage bill, we must still inquire why a majority in the council and the House voted in favor of it. Again, Governor Hoyt's explanation casts some light on the matter. Councilman Bright, although a political novice, by this account showed a remarkable degree of adroitness in maneuvering the bill through.

> Thus he said to the Democrats: "We have a Republican Governor and a Democratic Assembly. Now, then, if we can carry this bill through the Assembly and the Governor vetoes it, we shall have made a point, you know; we shall have shown our liberality and lost nothing. But keep still; don't say anything about it." They promised. He then went to the Republicans and told them that the Democrats were going to support his measure, and that if *they* did not want to lose capital they had better vote for it too. He didn't think there would be enough of them to carry it, but the vote would be on record and thus defeat the game of the other party. And they likewise agreed to vote for it. So, when the bill came to a vote it went right through! The members looked at each other in astonishment, for they hadn't intended to do it, *quite.* Then they laughed, and said it was a good joke, but they had "got the Governor in a fix." So the bill went, in the course of time, to John A. Campbell, who was then Governor—the first Governor of the Territory of Wyoming—and he promptly signed it! [15]

The difficulty with Governor Hoyt's statement is that there is no record of any Republicans being in the first territorial assembly whom Bright could have connived with. In the first territorial legislature the Democrats held every seat in both the council and the House. A far more plausible explanation is given by Justice Kingman.

> I ought to say distinctly, that Mr. Bright was himself fully and firmly convinced of the justice and policy of his bill, and gave his whole energy and influence to secure its passage; he secured some members by agreeing to support their pet schemes in return, and some he won over by even less creditable means. He got some votes by admitting that the governor would veto the bill (and it was generally understood that he would), insisting at the same time, that it would give the Democrats an advantage in future elections by showing that they were in favor of liberal measures while the Republican governor and the Republican party were opposed to them. *The favorite argument, however, and by far the most effective was this:* it would prove a great advertisement, would make a great deal of talk, and attract attention to the legislature, and the territory, more effectually than anything else. The bill was finally passed and sent to the governor. I must add, however, that many letters were written from different parts of the territory, and particularly by the women, to members of the legislature urging its passage and approving its object.[16]

Four factors thus emerge as instrumental in achieving the passage of the woman suffrage bill according to Justice Kingman: there was the possible party advantage to be gained by supporting the bill; there was a certain amount of logrolling which secured votes not otherwise available; there was the earnest persuasion of some women; but the most important factor in support of woman suffrage was its public relations value *outside* the state.

Wyoming, in its infancy as a territory, had had a consid-

erable amount of the bad publicity that was normally associated with the frontier shortly after the Civil War. It was
Indian country, criss-crossed by the wagon ruts of the pioneers who had made their way west to Oregon and California, and by the roads of the miners who had struck it
rich at South Pass. Early Wyoming held a strange mixture
of people: Chinese coolies who had set down the railroad
ties eastward from Sacramento; Irishmen who had walked
hundreds of miles westward putting down the tracks from
Omaha; newly emancipated Negroes seeking a place to
enjoy their freedom; Union troops employed to protect
the construction workers on the railroad, bored now with
garrison duty; former Confederate soldiers drifting westward from a devasted homeland, looking for a new start.
To a reader of the New York *Post,* or a farmer working the
flatlands of central Illinois, the dispatches which came in
from Wyoming could hardly be an inducement to settle
there, let alone settle with one's wife, sisters, or daughters.
Women were a scarce commodity in Wyoming. It may be
conjectured that the legislature resorted to special inducements to help alleviate this shortage, granting privi-
leges in much the same manner in which states have his-
torically sought to attract businesses by offering them special benefits. Early in our national history noneconomic
incentives such as religious freedom had been employed to
attract immigrants. Wyoming's pioneering legislation in
woman's rights may in this sense be seen as something of a
measure of its need for women settlers.

   The woman suffrage bill, having been passed by a sol-
idly Democratic legislature, went to the appointed governor for his signature. He was, as were the other territorial
officers—the secretaries, auditors, and justices of the supreme court—a Grant appointee and a Republican. Why

did Governor Campbell sign this Democratic bill? Here
again Justice Kingman's account is instructive.

> On receipt of the bill, the governor was in great doubt
> what course to take. He was inclined to veto it, and had
> so expressed himself; but he did not like to take the re-
> sponsibility of offending the women in the territory, or of
> placing the Republican party in open hostility to a meas-
> ure which he saw might become of political force and im-
> portance. I remember well an interview that Chief-Justice
> Howe and myself had with him at that time, in which we
> discussed the policy of the bill, and both of us urged him
> to sign it with all the arguments we could command.
> After a protracted consultation we left him still doubtful
> what he would do. But in the end he signed it, and drew
> upon himself the bitter curses of those Democrats who
> had voted for the bill with the expectation that he would
> veto it. From this time onward, the measure became
> rather a Republican than a Democratic principle, and
> found more of its friends in the former party, and more of
> its enemies in the latter.[17]

*

So the woman suffrage act of Wyoming territory became
law, December 10, 1869. The act, in itself a short and simple statement, was quite comprehensive in scope and soon
brought about three results which focused newspaper attention on Wyoming. First, it made possible the appointment of Mrs. Esther Morris, that redoubtable six-foot
suffragette, as the first woman justice of the peace, in the
gold-boom town of South Pass City. "She tried between
thirty and forty cases, and decided them so acceptably that
not one of them was appealed to a higher court," Justice
Kingman reports.[18] Second, it brought about the calling
of women for jury duty. Women in Wyoming constituted

a small minority, and as voters posed no immediate threat to the *status quo;* as members of grand and petit juries they constituted a threat, on the side of law and order, out of all proportion to their numbers. Single men, or those without their families, were likely to be soldiers of fortune, opportunists eager to strike their riches and move on. Married women, however, were the community builders par excellence, eager to put down roots, to make the streets safe from injury and disrespect, to build churches and erect schools, and to restore as far as possible the niceties and amenities of the civilized communities they had left behind. In March 1870, the first women jurors were drawn for the district court which met at Laramie. On this occasion a large number of women were drawn for grand and petit jurors. "As this was not done by the friends of woman suffrage," Justice Kingman reports, "there was evidently an intention of making the whole subject odious and ridiculous, and giving it a death-blow at the outset." [19] Assured, however, of the protection of the court, all but one of the women drawn for jury duty agreed to serve, and the first grand jury in Albany County (Laramie) was composed of six women and nine men, of whom Justice Kingman wrote, "they became such a terror to evil-doers that a stampede began among them and very many left the town forever." [20]

The first legislature had enacted a Sunday-closing law which had been commonly disregarded in Laramie, because the saloons normally had their best day on Sunday. This grand jury brought in indictments against every saloon in Laramie. Henceforth, the Sunday law was observed by the saloons and, according to Justice Kingman, "so great has been the change in that town in the habits of the people and the quiet appearance of the streets on Sunday, as compared with other towns in the territory, that it has been nick-named the *'Puritan town'* of Wyoming. . . ." [21]

It would seem safe to characterize the influence of civically active women on early Wyoming justice as essentially Puritan in character. Some women had, according to Mrs. Susan B. Anthony, argued in support of the woman suffrage bill to the governor partly on the grounds that it would "compel the men to observe the decencies of life." By all accounts, the official presence of decent women in the courtroom had precisely this effect. According to Chief Justice J. H. Howe, in a letter written in April 1870, to the Chicago *Legal News:* "They were educated, cultivated eastern ladies, who are an honor to their sex. They have, with true womanly devotion, left their homes of comfort in the States to share the fortunes of their husbands and brothers in the far West and to aid them in founding a new State beyond the Missouri." [22]

Furthermore, he noted (and Justice Kingman on a separate occasion corroborated), the official presence of these women in the courtroom gave a degree of dignity to the proceedings which was rare for Wyoming in those days. "The presence of these ladies in court secured the most perfect decorum and propriety of conduct, and the gentlemen of the bar and others vied with each other in their courteous and respectful demeanor toward the ladies and the court." [23] Such a salutary effect upon the processes of justice was clearly welcomed by those whose responsibility it was to see that the law was fairly enforced, but such an enthusiastic endorsement as that given by Chief Justice Hoyt is indeed impressive. In his tribute to the woman jurors he stated:

> With all my prejudices against the policy, I am under conscientious obligations to say that these women

acquitted themselves with such dignity, decorm, propriety of conduct and intelligence as to win the
admiration of every fair-minded citizen of Wyoming.
They were careful, painstaking, intelligent and conscien-
tious. They were firm and resolute for the right established by the law and the testimony. Their verdicts were
right, and, after three or four criminal trials, the lawyers
engaged in defending persons accused of crime began to
avail themselves of the right of peremptory challenge to
get rid of the female jurors, who were too much in favor
of enforcing the laws and punishing crime to suit the interests of their clients. After the grand jury had been in
session two days, the dance-house keepers, gamblers and
demi-monde fled out of the city in dismay, to escape the
indictment of women grand jurors! In short I have never,
in twenty-five years of constant experience in the courts of
the country, seen more faithful, intelligent and resolutely
honest grand and petit juries than these.[24]

Finally, in addition to making possible the appointment
of woman jurors and a few justices of the peace, the new
act fulfilled its primary and ostensible purpose, the establishment of woman suffrage in Wyoming.

＊

It is interesting to consider, in retrospect, what political
consequences we might expect in a frontier society upon
this extension of the franchise to women. Would the individual legislators who had voted for the extension of the
franchise be rewarded with re-election, and those who had
opposed it be punished by defeat in a demonstration of
support for the suffrage movement? Would the Democratic
party—since all members of the first territorial legislature
were Democrats—become even more firmly entrenched in
power as the party of suffrage extension? What of the im-

pact on the total vote in the territory? Would it increase greatly, now that women were added to the roll of eligible voters. Curiously, none of these consequences took place.

Of the nine members of the council and the twelve members of the House in the first legislature, only two stood for re-election. One of these, council member George Wardman, was absent when the woman suffrage vote was taken in the council. He was defeated for re-election. House member Ben Sheeks, who had been the most vigorous opponent of woman suffrage in the chamber, was re-elected.

Elections for the second legislature took place in September 1871. Democrats on the council dropped from nine to five; the House was increased in size to thirteen seats, of which the Republicans won four. Personal popularity may have been as much an issue here as party identification. However, Laramie County, which contained the largest town in the territory, Cheyenne, elected all three of the Democratic candidates for the House and two out of three candidates for the council. But in Albany County, which contained the second-largest town, Laramie, the Democrats elected only one out of three seats in the House and failed to hold either of the two seats in the council.

What was apparently taking place may become clearer if we look at the vote totals for the first five years of Wyoming's existence as an organized territory. The special census taken in 1869 showed a total population of 8014. Yet in Wyoming's first election (prior, of course, to woman suffrage), an extraordinarily high total of 5264 votes were cast.[25] Since the total vote cast for council members corresponds closely to the territorial-wide vote for the delegate to Congress, this high vote would not seem due to a tabulation error. Henceforth, the delegate to Congress would be elected in even years and the territorial legislature in odd-numbered years. Thus, another election for delegate to Congress took place in 1870, at a time when the regular census now showed the territorial population to have increased by almost 14 per cent. This time the Democratic incumbent failed to be re-elected, and a Republican associate justice of the territorial supreme court won. However, the vote dropped off sharply to only 3109, a reduction of approximately 41 per cent.

There is the possibility that the sharp decline in voting in 1870 might be attributed to a lack of interest in elections in which the legislature was not elected.[26] This possibility would appear unreasonable, however, in view of the great party interest in national elections held in the even years. Unfortunately, the data are not available from Albany County (containing Laramie) for the election of 1871, so we cannot compare vote totals of 1870 with those of 1871. However, the voting turnout of 1870 would seem to be confirmed by a comparison in Laramie County (containing Cheyenne) of the years 1869 to 1874. In 1869, the

TABLE I

Year	Total Census	Laramie County Vote (Cheyenne)		Territorial Total Vote	
		Delegate	Council	Delegate	Council
1869	8014	1608	—	5264	5047
1870	9118	860	—	3109	—
1871	—	—	611	—	—
1872	—	1090	—	3594	—
1873	—	—	1072	—	3755
1874	—	1548	—	4433	—

Laramie County vote for delegate to Congress was 1608 [27]; in 1870 this dropped to 860; in 1871 the Laramie County voter turnout for council members dropped further to 611; in 1874 the delegate vote rose to 1548.

The reduction in voting following the enactment of woman suffrage is clearly confirmed by all available data. It is summarized in Table I.[28]

To find some explanation for this surprising development in Wyoming, we may turn again to the report on woman suffrage given by Justice Kingman. His account, while admittedly biased, reveals at least a part of the social outlook that motivated the constituency just enlarged by woman suffrage.

The first election under the woman suffrage law was held in September, 1870, for the election of a delegate to congress, and county officers. There was an exciting canvass, and both parties applied to the whiskey shops, as before, supposing, they would wield the political power of the territory, and that not enough women would vote to influence the result. The morning of election came, but did not bring the usual scenes around the polls. A few women came out early to vote, and the crowd kept entirely out of sight. There was plenty of drinking and noise at the saloons, but the men would not remain, after voting, around the polls. *It seemed more like Sunday than election day.* Even the negro men and women voted without objection or disturbance. Quite a number of women voted during the day, at least in all the larger towns, but apprehension of a repetition of the scenes of the former election and doubt as to the proper course for them to pursue, kept very many from voting. The result was a great disappointment all around. The election had passed off with unexpected quiet, and order had everywhere prevailed. The whiskey shops had been beaten and their favorite candidate for congress, although he had spent several thousand dollars to secure an election, was left out in the cold.[29]

Justice Kingman's testimony on this first election in Wyoming after the passage of woman suffrage was in part corroborated by a letter written to the *Laramie Sentinel* by a Boston clergyman who had arrived in Laramie in time to witness this election. He had, he declared, been open-minded on the issue of woman suffrage until he had witnessed this election; henceforth he was a supporter of the movement.

And I was compelled to allow that in this new country, supposed at that time to be infested by hordes of cut-throats, gamblers and abandoned characters, I had witnessed a more quiet election than it had been my fortune to see in the quiet towns of Vermont. I saw ladies attended by their husbands, brothers, or sweethearts, ride to the places of voting, and alight in the midst of a silent crowd, and pass through an open space to the polls, depositing their votes with no more exposure to insult or injury than they would expect on visiting a grocery store or meat-market. Indeed, they were much safer here, every man of their party was pledged to shield them, while every member of the other party feared the influence of any signs of disrespect.

And the next day I sent my impressions to an eastern paper, declaring myself convinced *that woman's presence at the polls would elevate the tone of public sentiment there as it does in Churches, the social hall, or any other place.* . . .

Without reference to party issues, I noticed that a majority of women voted for men of the most temperate habits, thus insuring success to the party of law and order.[30]

These accounts would seem to explain the curious drop-off of ballots cast following the enactment of woman suffrage. The election of 1870 was apparently decorous, quiet, sober, and probably honest; evidently, the election of 1869 had been characterized by none of these qualities. Evidently, also, woman suffrage had a greater impact on the election outside the polling booths than inside them. As voters, women possessed little numerical strength (there were fewer than 1500 women over the age of 21 in 1870); but as symbols of civilization they seemed to impose, by their very presence, a restraint upon the political proceedings. Apparently, the mere presence of the ladies brought to the polls a rare combination of civility and chagrin.

*

The importance of Wyoming women in this symbolic role of civilizers of the frontier accords well with their interest in establishing churches and schools and in bringing the standards of civility at least up to the level of the homes they had left behind further east. By and large, it would seem safe to assert that women have been the traditional carriers of primary education, of the cultural amenities of civilizations, and of religion. The civilizing role of the churches along the frontier cannot be overestimated. "Of all the agencies utilized by man in maintaining traditional civilization on the successive frontiers in America," Louis B. Wright has noted, "it should now be abundantly clear that none was more effective than organized religion." [31] Furthermore, Wright observed:

> The role of the churches in maintaining decorum, decency, and morality on the turbulent frontier goes without saying. One of their essential functions was to

serve as moral courts and to enforce discipline in a region where the better element had to be constantly on guard against license and lawlessness. . . . Their notions of conquering the powers of evil did not stop with victory in the realm of morality. Civilization included education, cultivation, and good manners, and the churches labored persistently on the side of the angels of cultural light. Their success was far greater than cynics have been willing to admit. The churches always fought to re-establish traditional civilization and their conservatism usually prevailed.[32]

Just as women constituted the backbone of the churches along the frontier, their mere presence at public polling booths constituted a reminder of the community-building ethic in the primitive society.

If it may be argued that the woman suffrage vote including male supporters as well as women was essentially a community-building vote, it may equally be hypothesized that it was probably an antisaloon, if not outright prohibition, vote; and that in party orientation it was Republican. With the exception of the Cleveland appointees, the appointed territorial power structure—if one may term the federally appointed governors, secretaries, auditors, justices of the supreme court, and U.S. marshals such—were Republican. During the years 1869–90, however, the territorial council was basically Democratic, while the House of Representatives was quite evenly divided between the parties. Of the 127 councilmen who were elected during this period, some 77 were Democrats. Of the 238 members of the House, some 123 were Democratic. During the post-Civil War period, in which the Republican party was largely identified with the advancement of the West, this popular Democratic strength in Wyoming is rather surprising. It is perhaps explainable by the great westward migration which took place after the Civil War of Scotch, English and Irish immigrants moving westward along the railroad to the new homesteads, and the sheep and cattle ranches; of Southerners of similar ancestry moving into lands of new opportunities. Both groups had sympathetic ties with the Democratic party. A check of over 350 names of the members of the territorial legislatures reveals hardly a dozen which are not English, Scotch, or Irish in origin. If we pick, at random, the C's from the House of Representatives, they read: Cahill, Caldwell, Carter, Castle, Clark, Coad, Coates, Congdon, Conley, Conroy, Craig, Crawford, Cumock, Curran, Currier. Or the W's from the Council: Wardman, Warren, Whipple, Whitehead, Whittier, Wilson, Wright.[33] United States citizenship was not required for voting since alien residents could vote as long as they had declared their intention of becoming citizens. According to the Census of 1870 some 62 per cent (5605) of the residents of Wyoming were native Americans. Some 3513 were foreign-born. Community building in Wyoming thus took place simultaneously with "Americanizing"—in political processes, customs, and ethics—nearly 40 per cent of the population. This Americanization process, however, drew typically upon a norm of an American which, as Louis B. Wright observed, "had a prototype across the seas who was responsible for the American's language, his basic laws, his fundamental liberties, and much of his manners, customs, and social attitudes. That prototype was British, and primarily English. The English tradition was the strongest element of civilization on the successive frontiers." [34]

The ratio of American-born males to foreign-born males in Wyoming (1870) was nearly 4 : 3 (4258 : 2961); but the ratio of American-born females to foreign-born females was nearly 3 : 1 (1347 : 552). If we take the issue of the saloon alone, there must have been something of a gravitational pull of the Republican party on the native American women paralleling the pull of the Democratic party on the Irish-born settlers. Increasingly, and probably unconsciously, the Republican party was developing into the party of the white, Anglo-Saxon, Protestant; and within this broad ethic, the party of proclaimed moral virtue. It was still a long way from becoming the party of prohibition, but the seeds were there for later development. It was implicit in the speeches of the eastern suffragettes that the Republican party was the party of law and order, that women were for law and order and opposed to vice, and that the starting place of vice was the saloon. These sentiments were subscribed to by some of the supporters of woman suffrage in Wyoming, as may be seen by some of the testimony in behalf of woman suffrage given by Justice Kingman, if not by the purported opposition to woman suffrage attributed to saloon keepers. The saloon was, however, a basic social institution in early Wyoming history. As the inn or tavern had been to the seventeenth-century colonists a refuge for the traveler, a center of conviviality for the lonely, a plotting place for political conspirators, so was the nineteenth-century saloon a socializing force in the frontier community. It was a center for exchanging stories, for learning customs and names in the community, a place for the surplus male population of the territory to gather and to plan for the future. The saloon was by its very existence a potential cell of politics. But it would seem safe to assume that its politics was more largely concerned with the necessities of survival in the present than with community building for the future. The saloon was, unabashedly, undomesticatedly male in its social orientation; it was inevitably a natural foe of woman suffrage and the social ethic implicit in that movement. It was not surprising, therefore, that as the woman suffrage movement veered Republican, the saloon advocates veered Democratic.

*

The election of 1871, the second since the passage of woman suffrage, was the first opportunity for women to vote for members of the territorial legislature. Like the election of 1870, it was apparently orderly. Again we may turn to the testimony of Republican Justice Kingman: "A much larger number of women voted at this election than at the former one, but quite a number failed or refused to take part in it. . . . The Republicans had shown an unexpected strength and had returned several members to each House, although it was quite certain that some of the Democrats were indebted to the women for their success." It was at this juncture in Wyoming history that the Laramie (Albany County) grand jury, with its six women and nine men, had indicted the saloon keepers of the city for failure to abide by the Sunday law. Naturally, the saloon keepers responded by organizing an effort to repeal the Sunday law. "This aroused the women," Kingman wrote, "and they came out in force; many who had declined to vote before not only voted, but went round and induced others to do the same." [35] Apparently this mobilization of what must not have been over 300 women was politically successful, for the Democrats failed to place either of their two candidates in the council, and won only one of three seats in the House. Unfortunately, it is the figures for this election in Albany County which are missing, so we cannot judge how close it was and what possible difference the women's vote may have made.

These Republican victories were crucial to the cause of woman suffrage, however, for the election brought four Republicans to the council and four Republicans to the House; they were outvoted by five Democrats in the council and nine Democrats in the House. In this second territorial legislature a concerted effort was made by the Democrats to repeal woman suffrage, which, they believed, had only added to the strength of their opponents. On November 16, 1871, a Democratically sponsored bill repealing woman suffrage was introduced in the House; the following day it passed by the overwhelming vote of 9 ayes, 3 nays, with 1 absent. One Republican in the House defected to the opposition. The next day the bill was sent to the council where, on November 20, it swept through, unopposed: 8 ayes, 0 nays with 1 absent. Three Republicans (actually, 2 Republicans, 1 People's party) defected to the opposition. Governor Campbell, however, vetoed the bill with an impressive and cogent statement (occupying ten pages of the *Journal*). Returned to the House of Representatives, the bill was passed anew over the governor's veto, 9 to 2, with two members absent. This time, again, one Republican defected to the opposition, the other three Republicans being either opposed or in one case absent. Thus the House overrode the governor's veto. On December 14, the Council voted to override the veto, but mustered only a 5–4 vote, one vote short of the necessary two thirds. One Republican defected to the opposition; but one Democrat defected on this vote to the Republicans.[36] This vote was the last legislative effort to repeal woman suffrage in Wyoming Territory; and the territorial statute remained in effect until it was superseded by the state constitution of 1890, which contained its own woman suffrage provision.

*

Few sagas of the pioneer settlers are more impressively heroic than those of the community builders of Wyoming. Men and women from the eastern seaboard states had to journey some two thousand miles to find a land very like the wilderness grandeur described earlier by Francis Parkman.

> There was a plain before us, totally barren and thickly peopled in many parts with prairie-dogs, who sat at the mouths of their burrows and yelped at us as we passed. The plain, as we thought, was about six miles wide; but it cost us two hours to cross it. Then another mountain range rose before us. From the dense bushes that clothed the steeps for a thousand feet shot up black crags, all leaning one way, and shattered by storms and thunder into grim and threatening shapes. As we entered a narrow passage on the trail of the Indians, they impended frightfully above our heads.
>
> Our course was through thick woods, in the shade and sunlight of overhanging boughs. As we wound from side to side of the passage, to avoid its obstructions, we could see at intervals, through the foliage, the awful forms of the gigantic cliffs, that seemed to hem us in on the right and on the left, before and behind.[37]

Men and women from the fertile flatlands of Illinois, Indiana, and Ohio, and from further east, from New York and Pennsylvania and Vermont, pushed westward across the great prairie to the high plains of Wyoming to bring out of the barren soil the uncertain harvest of what came

to be called "dry farming." Yet nature was not the worst
enemy to these early settlers. The community builders had
to cope with what was inevitably an indifferent, if not outright hostile, social environment which resulted from the
very nature of life in what was predominately a mining region.

As a mining region, a fabled El Dorado, Wyoming attracted a horde of soldiers of fortune, nomadic bachelors,
who lived daily in the promise that below the crust of to-
morrow's digging, or in the dregs of the pan after the next
one, would be fabulous riches of gold or shining silver.
The small percentage who struck it rich kept up the fever
of the many who squandered their substance, their health
and, for some, their lives. These men were, at bottom,
gamblers. They came to get but not to give. They were in-
dividualists; asocial rather than antisocial. The building of
communities was of little concern to them except as a possible restraint upon their activities. They were essentially
nomadic, moving from stream to stream, from hill to hill,
from county to county. Their style of life was totally opposed to that of the settler. They came without women or
children; they had little concern with the social necessities
of law and order; they had no permanent interests in the
community, for if they were lucky they took their win-
nings and moved on. These itinerants, a large part of Wyoming's sparse population, presented a problem which
only increased with the coming of the cowboy trailing his
herds into a new pasture.

Miners and cowboys, however, were not the only members of the itinerant population. Wyoming was, typically,
but a point in passage in a man's career, not a home to be
prepared for grandchildren. The federally-appointed officers of the territory served their terms and then moved on

to other places and other occupations. Of the eight men appointed to the office of governor of the territory, only two clearly remained identified with the territory or state for the rest of their careers; of the sixteen territorial supreme court justices, only four continued their careers in Wyoming. Of the 127 men elected to the territorial council, only 15 were re-elected to office; of the 238 elected members of the territorial House of Representatives, only 20 were re-elected to office. It would seem reasonable to suppose that such an exceptionally high rate of political turnover in the territorial legislature must have been due in part to the mobility of the officeholders, as well as to the rapidly changing composition of the constituency.

To build a viable political community incorporating a respect for the processes of law and government in this mobile social setting must have imposed extraordinary demands upon the stable elements of the community, the ranchers, the businessmen, the farmers, the married householders, and those with a responsibility for female dependents under their roof. Woman suffrage, in all probability, was the political instrument of the community builders, for potentially it doubled the vote of the responsible householder, when compared with the unreliable, nomadic bachelor. It provided a stable nucleus of voting strength which could in time assist and protect the process of civilizing the frontier.

What now, we may inquire, was the relationship of woman suffrage to the frontier in Wyoming, and of both to the equalitarianism expressed in the constitution of 1890? The enactment of woman suffrage by the first territorial legislature was the result of a cleverness of strategy which produced not a genuine majority consensus but merely, by ironic chance, approval. In its original intro-

duction by Councilman Bright, and in its final signing by
Governor Campbell, there was doubtless sincerity, but in
between there was clearly a large element of political chi-
canery. In this new territory, there were no highly organized political forces which effectively controlled the legislature. Frontier conditions furthered its enactment only to
the extent that a small political group in a highly disorgan-
ized territory could legislate, unchallenged, unusual stat-
utes. Once enactment took place, however, vested interests
arose to ensure its operation. It was at this stage that
woman suffrage took on its predominantly Republican
complexion in a predominantly Democratic territory,
picked up support from the antisaloon people, and it is
suggested here, became an instrument of the community
builders. It is further suggested that this early woman
suffrage movement was not a product of frontier equalitarianism but in some respects its very antithesis. It was a
movement related to frontier conditions only to the extent
that it wished to ameliorate these conditions and impose
instead a respect for law and order and the civilities and
amenities of established communities. Woman suffrage was
in this sense a civilized reaction to frontier rowdiness.

The early record of women at the polls or in the jury
boxes seems to bear this out. Though men conquered the
wilderness, women made it inhabitable. Women, in scarce
supply in early Wyoming, were respected at the polls and
in the courtrooms not because they were politically equal
but because they were—quite simply—women, and as
such were symbols of home and civilization, whether as
wives, mothers, daughters or sisters. Their very presence
was in some fashion a civilizing agent.

Once set in motion, however, civilizing forces produced
a social momentum of their own as a new political rela-

tionship between the sexes was taught to a new generation of children in an effective school program. By 1890, when Wyoming was admitted to statehood, the first children that had been born in the territory were 21 years old. The broad equal-rights guarantees of the Wyoming constitution of 1890 were written for a vastly different type of political constituency than that which was present in the territory in 1869. We must therefore not confuse the constitutional guarantees of 1890, and the social and political forces which endorsed them, with the situation which existed at the earlier age. In conclusion, it may be said that the same social forces which were at work in Utah to sustain a civilization were at work in Wyoming to achieve one. In both cases these social forces sought to establish the norms of community behavior usually associated with the term "the Puritan ethic." These norms included order, temperance, honesty, and an extraordinary sense of calling or divine mission in the process of community building. The efforts to establish the Puritan ethic as the controlling political force was basic to the coming of woman suffrage to these territories.

CHAPTER IV

The Hostile "They"

> There is an enemy of the homes of this nation and that enemy is drunkenness. Every one connected with the gambling house, the brothel and the saloon works and votes solidly against the enfranchisement of women, and, I say, if you believe in chastity, if you believe in honesty and integrity, then do what the enemy wants you not to do, which is to take the necessary steps to put the ballot in the hands of women.
>
> Susan B. Anthony

By the turn of the century, not only had the status of women in America reached a new high, but the social revolution that underlay this improved status was proceding at such a pace that achievement of the goal of equal justice for women could realistically be expected early in the twentieth century. A fourth volume of over 1000 pages in the compendious *History of Woman Suffrage* was required simply to cover the activity of the period from 1884 to 1900. The volume prophesied as much as it recorded the past. The new editors, Susan B. Anthony and Ida Husted Harper, who had now relieved the venerable Elizabeth Cady Stanton of this task, wrote:

If the first organized demand for the rights of women— made at the memorable convention of Seneca Falls, N.Y.,

78

in 1848—had omitted the one for the franchise, those who made it would have lived to see all granted. It asked for woman the right to have personal freedom, to acquire an education, to earn a living, to claim her wages, to own property, to make contract, to bring suit, to testify in court, to obtain a divorce for just cause, to possess her children, to claim a fair share of the accumulations during marriage.[1]

Although in 1848 virtually all of these rights were denied by all of the states, at the turn of the century, no state denied all of these rights and in many states all of them were honored. The editors happily noted: "For the past half century there has been a steady advance in the direction of equal rights for women. . . . Enough has been accomplished in all of the above lines to make it absolutely certain that within a few years women everywhere in the United States will enjoy entire equality of legal, civil and social rights." [2]

When such remarkable progress in the cause of women's rights had been made in the previous half-century in all areas other than that of the franchise, why was it that the political change in the electorate, the simple act of enfranchising women, was so difficult to accomplish? In the view of the *History's* editors, there were many reasons which, combined in their effect, caused the glacierlike progress of the woman suffrage movement. The most important reason, they felt, was in the states a constitutional change was required to bring about woman suffrage, while other rights of women rested upon simple legislative enactment. Thus, a constitutional majority of voters at a referendum was required. In many states this meant not a simple majority of those voting on the question but a majority of the largest vote cast at the election on any issue or for any office. "No class of men could get any electoral right whatever," the editors realistically observed, "if it depended wholly on the consent of another class whose interests supposedly lay in withholding it. Political, not moral influence removed the property restrictions from the suffrage in order to build up a great party—the Democratic—which because of its enfranchisement of wage-earning men has received their support for eighty years." [3] Negro enfranchisement, in turn, could not be brought about through individual state constitutional changes even in antislavery, Republican states like Kansas; the Fifteenth Amendment received the necessary ratification in the states

> . . . only because it was positively certain that through this action an immense addition would be made to the Republican electorate. Now after a lapse of thirty years this same party looks on unmoved at the violation of these amendments in every Southern State because it is believed that thus there can be, through white suffrage, the building up of the party in that section which the colored vote has not been able to accomplish.[4]

Yet, the question remains, whose interest lay in denying the vote to women; whom did the National-American Woman Suffrage Association perceive to be their hostile "they"? In their opinion, the traditional party bosses and leaders of the dominant Republican and Democratic parties were "they" figures; and in this view we catch something of the flavor of the reform-minded, progressive outlook that would soon be significant in American politics. In a review of the efforts to influence the platform committees of the various political parties to endorse woman suffrage, Suffrage Association officers noted that, ever since 1868, suffragette representations at national conventions of all the parties had been made, with very disappointing results. The Republican party, in 1872 and 1876, adopted vague statements in its platforms endorsing additional rights for women. The Republican platforms of 1880–92 were silent on the subject. In 1896 that platform declared: "We favor the admission of women to wider spheres of usefulness, and welcome their cooperation in rescuing the country from Democratic mismanagement and Populist misrule." [5] The editors caustically added, "No Democratic national platform ever has recognized so much as the existence of women, in all its grandiloquent declarations of, the 'rights of the masses,' the 'equality of the people,' the 'sovereignty of the individual' and the 'powers inherent in a democracy'." [6]

When the Populist party held its Omaha convention in 1892, Susan B. Anthony and Anna Howard Shaw sallied forth "full of joy and hope," only to be refused permission even to appear before the resolutions committee. Although the Populists accorded a greater role to women on political committees, and as organizers and speakers, once they joined with the Democrats in 1896, "the political rights of women were hopelessly lost in the shuffle." "By 1900," the editors noted, "the organization was thoroughly under Democratic control, and the expectations of women to secure their enfranchisement through this 'party of the people,' created to reform all abuses and abolish all unjust discriminations, vanished forever." [7]

Inevitably, perhaps, woman suffrage fared better in the platforms of the lesser parties which needed all the support they could get. Thus, the Prohibition party, supported by the Woman's Christian Temperance Union, consistently endorsed woman suffrage except in 1896. Support was also given by "the Greenback party, the Labor party, the various Socialist parties," although the editors commented: "Whether they would do so if strong enough to have any hope of electing their candidates must remain an open question until practically demonstrated." [8]

Major party leaders were opposed to woman suffrage partly because they could not be certain how women would vote. The Populist party helped bring about woman suffrage in Colorado in 1893; in the next election (with woman suffrage), the Populists were defeated. "Many consider that the principles of the Republican party in general would be more apt to commend themselves to women than those of the Democratic, but others believe that, so great is their antipathy to war and all its evils connected with it and the consequences following it, they would have opposed the party responsible for these during the past four years [1896–1900]." [9] While the "principles of the Republican Party" were left obscure, nevertheless the implication that women were antiwar and opposed to McKinley imperialism was made emphatic enough by the editors. (It was a foretaste of the voting record on peace of the suffragette and Congresswoman Jeannette Rankin.) In the election of 1900, with women voting in four states (Wyoming, Colorado, Idaho, and Utah), two states went Democratic and two Republican. "It may be accepted, however," the editors prudently noted, "as the most probable view that women will divide on the main issues in much the same proportion as men." [10] At this stage, no certain political advantage was apparent to a party leader to cause him to advocate woman suffrage. There were, however, certain disadvantages to woman suffrage which an astute party leader would be wise to assess.

Candidates who would be perfectly acceptable to men if they were sound on the political issues might be wholly repudiated by the women of their own party. If temperance and morality were made requisites, many leaders and officials who now hold high position would be permanently retired. These are all reasons which appeal to politicians in deferring the day of woman suffrage as long as possible.[11]

Clearly, behind the issue of woman suffrage was a conflict over social values in the community, a conflict which was as yet not clearly defined. By the turn of the century, women were increasingly coming to be looked upon as the custodians of public as well as private morality. It was the historical function of women in their role as mothers to impress their young with standards of moral conduct and good behavior; more and more, by the turn of the century, this task was further carried on by women in the classroom. Now, as a by-product of the women's rights movement, it was reaching more fully into the adult realm of public affairs. Inevitably, this emphasis on morality by the advocates of woman suffrage produced in the minds of some party leaders an image not unlike that of a Puritan scourge incarnate—and equally to be dreaded. When the editors could report, as after woman suffrage was enacted in Colorado that "every political party has banished liquor and tobacco from its headquarters, as desiring to win the women's support they are careful not to give offense," [12] it must have given Boston ward heelers cause for alarm and conjured up in Tammany Hall the specter of a visitation from reformist Anthony Comstock.

In addition to political leaders and party bosses the category of antagonists included the liquor and brewing companies, which the woman suffrage advocates saw as sinister forces that virtually controlled politics at every level of government.

> Each of the two dominant parties is largely controlled by what are known as the liquor interests. Their influence begins with the National Government, which receives from them billions of revenue; it extends to the States, to which they pay millions; to the cities, whose income they increase by hundreds of thousands; to the farmers, who find in breweries and distilleries the best market for their grain. There is no hamlet so small as not to be touched by their ramifications. No "trust" ever formed can compare with them in the power which they exercise. . . . They and the various institutions connected with them control millions of votes. They are among the largest contributors to political campaigns. There are few legislators who do not owe their election in a greater or less degree to the influence wielded by these liquor interests, which are positively, unanimously, and unalterably opposed to woman suffrage.[13]

Foremost in the ranks of the supporters of woman suffrage was the Woman's Christian Temperance Union, which had been organized in 1874 in order to fulfill this pledge: "I hereby solemnly promise, God helping me, to abstain from all distilled, fermented and malt liquors, including wine, beer and cider, and to employ all proper means to discourage the use of and traffic in the same." [14] This of course was not temperance but prohibition; and the various brewing and liquor interests could quite legitimately see themselves as threatened by the rising power of the W.C.T.U., which, under the organizing genius of Frances E. Willard, had established chapters in 10,000 towns and cities across the United States and in 1900 claimed a dues-paying membership of 300,000. The W.C.T.U. claimed credit for mandatory temperance instruction in the public schools as well as temperance teaching in the Sunday schools; Chautauqua gatherings provided opportunities for the W.C.T.U. to present its message. In the listings of national women's organizations in the *History of Woman Suffrage,* the W.C.T.U. was given the greatest amount of space. That the organization was concerned with far more than temperance is evident from a partial description of its activities:

> This organization has largely influenced the change in public sentiment in regard to social drinking, equal suffrage, equal purity for both sexes, equal remuneration for work equally well done, equal education, professional and industrial opportunities for women. It has been a chief factor in State campaigns for statutory prohibition, constitutional amendment, reform laws in general and those for the protection of women and children in particular, and in securing anti-gambling and anti-cigarette laws. It has been instrumental in raising the "age of protection" for girls in many States, [under the common law the age was 10 years] and in obtaining curfew laws in 400 towns and cities. It aided in securing the Anti-Canteen Amendment to the Army Bill [1900] which prohibits the sale of intoxicating liquors at all army posts. It helped to inaugurate police matrons who are now required in nearly all the large cities of the United States. It organized Mothers' Meetings in thirty-seven States before any other society took up the work. . . .
>
> The association protests against the legalizing of all crimes, especially those of prostitution and liquor selling.[15]

For solid support in the cause of secular "purity," the W.C.T.U. was a stout, formidable ally. There were many instances, as will appear later, in which supporters of woman suffrage were not supporters of prohibition, but ever since the Prohibition party—the first third party after the Civil War—had adopted a woman suffrage plank in its 1869 platform, there was a marked tendency, especially in the West, for supporters of prohibtion to support woman suffrage as an effective means of achieving their goal. It was this aspect of the relationship between prohibition and woman suffrage which the liquor and brewing interests found threatening. And they responded to the threat by opposing woman suffrage, as did the Wholesale Liquor Dealers' League in California in 1895, when it issued the following to saloon keepers, hotels, and grocers:

> At the election to be held on November 3, Constitutional Amendment No. Six, which gives the right to vote to women, will be voted on. It is to your interest and ours to vote against this amendment. We request and urge you to vote and work against it and do all you can to defeat it.[16]

In addition to the political bosses and the liquor interests, the category of opponents included the foreign-born. In state after state, according to the *History of Woman Suffrage,* whenever there was a referendum on woman suffrage the foreign-born were reported to vote against it. In South Dakota, for example, where the referendum on woman suffrage was defeated in 1890 by the overwhelming vote of 54,862 nays to 22,072 ayes, it was recorded: "There were 30,000 Russians, Poles, Scandinavians and other foreigners in the State, most of whom opposed woman suffrage." [17] In California, the Chinese were reported opposed to woman suffrage; in Iowa, it was reported that "The politics of that State is practically controlled by the great brewing interests and the balance of power rests in the German vote." [18] In 1880, Susan B. Anthony testified on behalf of woman suffrage before the U.S. Senate Judiciary Committee; in the course of her testimony she explained the cause of the recent (1877) defeat of the woman suffrage referendum in Colorado as follows:

In Colorado, at the close of the canvass, 6,666 men voted "Yes." Now, I am going to describe the men who voted "Yes." They were native-born white men, temperance men, cultivated, broad, generous, just men, men who think. On the other hand, 16,007 voted "No." Now, I am going to describe that class of voters. In the southern part of that State there are Mexicans, who speak the Spanish language. They put their wheat in circles on the ground with the heads out, and drive a mule around to thrash it. The vast population of Colorado is made up of that class of people. I was sent out to speak in a voting precinct having 200 voters; 150 of those voters were Mexican greasers, 40 of them foreign-born citizens, and just 10 of them were born in this country; and I was supposed to be competent to convert those men to let me have so much right in this Government as they had, when, unfortunately, the great majority of them could not understand a word that I said. . . .

Right in the file of the foreigners opposed to woman suffrage, educated under monarchical governments that do not comprehend our principles, whom I have seen traveling through the prairies of Iowa, or the prairies of Minnesota, are the Bohemians, Swedes, Norwegians, Germans, Irishmen, Mennonites; I have seen them riding on those magnificent loads of wheat with those magnificent Saxon horses, shining like glass on a sunny morning, every one of them going to vote "no" against woman suffrage. You cannot convert them; it is impossible. Now and then there is a whiskey manufacturer, drunkard, inebriate, libertine, and what we call a fast man, and a colored man, broad and generous enough to be willing to let women vote, to let his mother have her opinion counted as to whether there shall be license or no license, but the rank and file of all classes who wish to enjoy full license in what are termed the petty vices of men are pitted solid against the enfranchisement of women. Then, in addition to all these, there are, as you know, a few religious bigots left in the world who really believe that somehow or other if women are allowed to vote, Saint Paul would feel badly about it. . . . So when you put those best men of the nation having religion about everything except on this one question, whose prejudices control them, with all this vast mass of ignorant, uneducated, degraded population in this country, you make an overwhelming and insurmountable majority against the enfranchisement of women.[19]

The political bosses, the liquor interests, and the foreigners, all came together, of course, in the cities; and it was here that the advocates of woman suffrage found the going hardest. In the referendum in Colorado in 1893, all eyes were focused on Denver, since it was noted: "It is always in cities that reforms meet defeat, for there the opposing interests are better organized and more watchful."[20]

Denver, [it was reported by one chronicler of woman suffrage] presented an interesting social aspect at this time. It was as if the precursive tremor of a moral earthquake had been felt, and people, only half awake, did not know whether to seek safety in the house, or outside of it. Women especially were perplexed and inquiring, and it was observed that those in favor of asking a recognition of their rights in the new State, were the intelligent and leading ladies of the city. The wives of ministers, of con-

gressmen, of judges, the prominent members of Shake-
speare clubs, reading circles, the directors of charitable
institutions,—these were the ones who first ranged themselves on the side of equal rights. . . .[21]

In Oregon, in the referendum of 1900, it was reported that
"the measure in all probability would have carried had it
not been for the slum vote of Portland and Astoria. . . .
Twenty-one out of the thirty-three counties gave hand-
some majorities; one county was lost by one vote, one by
23 and one by 31." [22] Woman suffrage was not, however,
affected as much by class differences as by differences over
social values. At issue was a conflict over styles of life or
modes of existence. On one side was the older, conservative, rural, essentially Protestant and Puritan way of life
which the native-born liked to think of as typically American; on the other side was the new or "faster" style of life
that accompanied late nineteenth-century urbanization,
and was ostentatious, crude but sophisticated, and enthu-
siastically "wet." The former style drew its nourishment
from farms, small towns, and a traditional way of life; the
latter style was fed by mining, factories, immigrant labor,
and the new modes of wealth made possible by burgeoning
capitalism. In California, for example, in 1896 the woman
suffrage amendment was supported by the antiforeign and
anti-Catholic American Protective Association; it was defeated in an election which brought forth 247,454 votes on
the issue—110,355 ayes, 137,099 nays. According to the
History of Woman Suffrage, "Every county in Southern
California gave a majority for the amendment, Los Angeles County leading with 4,600." [23] However, a majority of
23,772 votes was cast against the amendment in San Francisco County, while another majority of 3,627 votes went
against the amendment in Alameda County (which in-

cluded Oakland, Alameda, and Berkeley). Since Berkeley voted in favor of the amendment, the defeat really came from San Francisco, Alameda, and Oakland. According to the chronicler, the result in Alameda "was a most unpleasant surprise, as the voters were principally Republicans and Populists, both of whom were pledged in the strongest possible manner in their county conventions to support the amendment, and every newspaper in the county had declared in favor of it." Furthermore, "Alameda is the banner Republican County and gave a good majority for the Republican ticket." [24] The implication here, and frequently throughout the various volumes of the *History,* was that the Republican party should provide the natural home for the woman suffrage movement.

However, to return to an analysis of the vote which defeated woman suffrage in California in 1896, it was evident that the opposition cut through all classes.

As it is almost universally insisted that woman suffrage amendments are defeated by the ballots of the ignorant, the vicious and the foreign born, an analysis of the vote in San Francisco, which contains more of these elements than all the rest of California, is of interest. Not one of the eighteen Assembly Districts was carried for the amendment and but one precinct in the whole city. It is not practicable to draw an exact dividing line between the best and the worst localities in any city, but possibly the 28th, or water front, district in San Francisco may come under the latter head and the 40th under the former. The vote on the amendment in the 28th was 355 ayes, 1,188 noes; in the 40th, 890 ayes, 2,681 noes, a larger percentage of opposition in the district containing the so-called best people. Districts 37, 39, 40, 41, 42, 43 would probably be designated the most aristocratic of the city. Their vote on the amendment was 5,189 ayes, 13,615 noes, an opposing majority of 8,426, or about 1,400 to the district. This left the remainder to be distributed among the other eighteen districts, including the ignorant, the vicious and the foreign born, with an average of less than 1,300 adverse votes in each district.

The proportion of this vote was duplicated in Oakland, the most aristocratic ward giving as large a negative majority as the one commonly designated "the slums." [25]

If there was more rhetoric than reality to the charge that the ignorant, the foreign-born, and the degenerate (often equated) were inevitably opponents of woman suffrage, it must be remembered that the leadership of the movement came from middle-class, native-born, educated women whose perception of the social order about them was largely shaped by their own backgrounds. They therefore resented being denied the ballot by those to whom they felt socially superior. In their view, they seemed to be threatened by a relative decline in political status at the very time that the status of women was rising in other fields of endeavor. At the very time when native-born women were founding organizations to preserve their status—the Daughters of the American Revolution in 1890, the Colonial Dames of America in 1890, the National Society of United States Daughters of 1812 in 1892, the United Daughters of the Confederacy in 1894—their social values were being threatened by a political system in which they could not participate.

*

A further analysis of the social factors involved in the woman suffrage movement was provided by Mrs. H. S.

Mendenhall of Georgetown, Colorado, only a few hours
after the referendum was voted upon (and defeated) there
in 1877:

> The Methodist men were for us; the Presbyterians and
> Episcopalians very fairly so, and the Roman Catholics
> were not all against us, some of the prominent members
> of that church working and voting for woman suffrage.
> The liquor interest went entirely against us, as far as I
> know.
>
> The observations of the day have led me to several gen-
> eral conclusions, to which, of course, exceptions exist: (1)
> married men will vote *for* suffrage if their wives appreci-
> ate its importance. (2) men without family ties, and espe-
> cially if they have associated with a bad class of women,
> will vote against it. (3) boys who have just reached their
> majority will vote against it more uniformly than any
> other class of men. We were treated with the utmost re-
> spect by all except the last class. Destitute of experience,
> and big with their own importance, these young sover-
> eigns will speak to a woman twice their years with a
> flippancy which the most ignorant foreigner of mature
> age would not use, and I have to-day been tempted to be-
> lieve that no one is fitted to exercise the American
> franchise under twenty-five years of age.[26]

The division along religious lines over woman suffrage
reflected not only the close association of the Methodists
with the temperance issue but equally the conflict in social
outlook in the late nineteenth century between the native-
born Americans and those foreign-born. The very wording
of the analysis quoted above implied an expectation the
Roman Catholics would be opposed to woman suffrage
and the note, almost of surprise, that they were not "all
against us" is similar to the shock noted above in Califor-

nia that the Republicans had not put woman suffrage over
in Alameda.

There was probably considerable justification for Mrs.
Mendenhall's observation in Colorado that married men
would vote for woman suffrage if their wives were in favor
of it. For in addition to the social forces and interests ac-
tively opposed to woman suffrage, the leaders of the movement recognized that they had a tremendous political
handicap to overcome: the general political apathy of the
average woman. It was difficult enough to cope with the
general opposition of the average man, who, it was observed, would have refused to allow women to enter the
universities and professions, to speak from public platforms or to control their own property, had these issues
been left to be determined by public vote. "To grant
woman an equality with man in the affairs of life," the editors of the *History* noted, "is contrary to every tradition,
every precedent, every inheritance, every instinct and
every teaching." [27] Yet these same issues would probably
have fared no better had they been decided upon by a majority of women themselves.

They are more conservative than men, because of the nar-
rowness and isolation of their lives, the subjection in
which they always have been held, the severe punishment
inflicted by society on those who dare step outside the
prescribed sphere, and, stronger than all, perhaps, their
religious tendencies through which it has been impressed
upon them that their subordinate position was assigned
by the Divine will and that to rebel against it is to defy
the Creator. In all the generations, Church, State and society have combined to retard the development of women,
with the inevitable result that those of every class are nar-

rower, more bigoted and less progressive than the men of that class.[28]

To put the case for woman suffrage before a majority of voters in the separate states was an almost certain invitation to defeat. The party bosses, the liquor and brewing interests, the uneducated, the foreign-born, apathetic and indifferent women, and men habituated to superior status coalesced into one enormous hostile "they" against whom, according to their sloganeers, enlightened and heroic women struggled. Late in the nineteenth century, it was noted, "a modern skepticism as to the supreme merit of a democratic government and a general disgust with the prevalent corruption" had come about which made the struggle to extend the franchise even more difficult than it might normally be. Such would be the case, however, until men saw,

> . . . that a real democracy has not as yet existed, but that the dangerous experiment has been made of enfranchising the vast proportion of crime, intemperance, immorality and dishonesty, and barring absolutely from the suffrage the great proportion of temperance, morality, religion and conscientiousness; that, in other words, the worst elements have been put into the ballot-box and the best elements kept out. This fatal mistake is even now beginning to dawn upon the minds of those who have cherished an ideal of the grandeur of a republic, and they dimly see that in woman lies the highest promise of its fulfillment. Those who fear the foreign vote will learn eventually that there are more American-born women in the United States than foreign-born men and women; and those who dread the ignorant vote will study the statistics and see that the percentage of illiteracy is much smaller among women than among men.[29]

Yet in spite of the opposition of the hostile "they," four western states adopted woman suffrage in the decade of the nineties. In two of these states, Wyoming (1890) and Utah (1896), there was only minor skirmishing at the respective constitutional conventions, for their long experience with woman suffrage as territories had accustomed their electorates to it. Upon achieving statehood, their constitutional provisions for woman suffrage went into effect. Idaho, admitted to statehood in 1890, and considerably populated by Mormons in its southern section, adopted a woman suffrage amendment in a referendum in 1896 by the overwhelming vote of 12,126 for, to 6282 against.[30] What seems to have been a contributing factor in this result was the fact that all the political parties—the Republican, Democratic, People's party, and Silver Republicans—endorsed woman suffrage. In Colorado, which adopted woman suffrage in 1893, the issue was more hotly contested in spite of its endorsement at various county conventions by the Republican, Democratic, Prohibition, and Populist parties. In a referendum in 1877, the issue had been defeated; now with the cause taken up by the Populists, who were at this time at the height of their power in Colorado, woman suffrage had the necessary political backing. Indeed it would appear that the Populists and the woman suffrage movement appealed to much the same type of voter. For example, in March 1893, the bill authorizing the suffrage amendment passed the Colorado House by 34 ayes and 27 nays. The ayes were composed of 22 Populists, 11 Republicans, and 1 Democrat. The nays were composed of 21 Republicans, 3 Democrats, and 3 Populists. In April the bill passed the Senate with 20 ayes and 10 nays. The ayes were composed of 12 Populists and 8 Republicans. The nays were composed of 5 Democrats, 4

Republicans, and 1 Populist. In November the referendum cleared with a popular vote of 35,798 for and 29,451 against, a margin of 6,347 votes.[31]

Mrs. Emily R. Meredith, who wrote the study of woman suffrage in Colorado for Volume IV of the *History,* offered the following explanations for the 1893 victory in that state. "First, it may be claimed that Western men have more than others of that spirit of chivalry of which the world has heard so much and seen so little." In effect, this was an element in what became Webb's theory of the Great Plains (discussed in Chapter 1). Second, Mrs. Meredith suggested, "there is less prejudice against and a stronger belief in equal rights in the newer communities." This was in effect a corroboration of Turner's frontier thesis (also discussed in Chapter 1). Yet it should be observed that both of these factors or conditions were presumably present in Colorado in 1877 when the proposition was defeated. The issue in 1893, however, had the support of the labor oganizations, which it had lacked in 1877. Perhaps of greatest relevance was Mrs. Meredith's third observation:

> The pressure of hard times, culminating in the panic of 1893, undoubtedly contributed to the success of the Populist Party, and to its influence the suffrage cause owes much. . . . It was in the counties giving Populist pluralities that the majority of 6,818 in favor of equal suffrage was found. The counties which went Republican and Democratic gave a majority of 471 against the measure.[32]

Woman suffrage was adopted in Colorado in 1893 not simply because it was recognized that women needed votes but because Populists needed voters and women constituted an untapped source of supply. The conjunction of Populism and woman suffrage, and the consequent reluctance of the major parties in Colorado and Idaho to oppose it, made possible the enactment of woman suffrage in these two states. This confluence of social ideals—of Populism and woman suffrage—was indicative of a fundamental conflict between differing social values that was taking place in America in the 1890's. In the forefront of this contest, according to Frederick Jackson Turner, were descendants of old New England stock struggling to preserve the ideals of their forefathers. "If New England looks with care at these men," Turner wrote, "she may recognize in them the familiar lineaments of the embattled farmers who fired the shot heard round the world. The continuous advance of this pioneer stock from New England has preserved for us the older type of the pioneer of frontier New England." And in a heroic vein Turner observed:

> In the arid West these pioneers have halted and have turned to perceive an altered nation and changed social ideals. They see the sharp contrast between their traditional idea of America, as the land of opportunity, the land of the self-made man, free from class distinctions and from the power of wealth, and the existing America, so unlike the earlier ideal. If we follow back the line of march of the Puritan farmer, we shall see how responsive he has always been to *isms,* and how persistently he has resisted encroachments on his ideals of individual opportunity and democracy. He is the prophet of the "higher law" in Kansas before the Civil War. He is the Prohibitionist of Iowa and Wisconsin, crying out against German customs as an invasion of his traditional ideals. He is the Granger of Wisconsin, passing restrictive railroad legislation. He is the Abolitionist, the Anti-mason, the Millerite,

the Woman Suffragist, the Spiritualist, the Mormon, of Western New York.[33]

Now when we compare Turner's exposition of the antecedents of the Populists, written in 1897, with an analysis of the social origins of the suffragettes, written by Carrie Chapman Catt and Nettie Shuler a quarter of a century later, we see that adherents of both causes shared a similar background and motivation.

> Until the closing years of the struggle, when the suffrage army grew vastly larger and was recruited from all classes, its leaders and members were women of American birth, education and ideals. A remarkable number were daughters of Revolutionary fathers and in their childhood homes had learned the meaning of political freedom and had inherited other ideas of progress. Such women, turning to the States to seek enfranchisement, were driven to beg their right to have their opinions counted from Negroes, newly emancipated, untrained, and from foreign-born voters, mainly uneducated, with views concerning women molded by European tradition. No other women in the world suffered such humiliation nor worked against such odds for their political liberty.
> Yet the woman suffrage movement in the United States was a movement of *the spirit of the Revolution which was striving to hold the nation to the ideals which won independence.*[34]

With the passing of Populism as an effective force in American politics, the woman suffrage movement lost its short-lived momentum. Not until the Progressive movement developed in 1910 would suffrage referendums be successful in other states. The woman suffrage movement thus had to await a further gathering of strength of the social forces of which it was itself a part.

CHAPTER V

Our Country

Liberty for *all* the people is coming out of the West.
Mabel Croft Deering

For fourteen years following the triumphs of 1896 the woman suffrage movement in the states met only a dreary succession of defeats. Then, between 1910 and 1914, the golden age of statewide woman suffrage took place in the West, and only in the West. In 1910 Washington, in 1911 California, in 1912 Oregon, Arizona, and Kansas, in 1914 Nevada and Montana established woman suffrage. Thus, by 1914 Kansas, all the West Coast states and all the Rocky Mountain states except New Mexico had woman suffrage. How may we account for this regional pattern? Was it indeed a fact that by 1914 this vast western expanse manifested a high degree of equalitarianism?

If the lesson of Wyoming and Utah correctly portended the subsequent course of the woman suffrage movement, then we might have expected its growth to come in those areas in which there was significant political support for what we may call here the correlative values of woman suffrage, values which it was understood could be more securely achieved or preserved by bringing the support of women voters to the cause. Woman suffrage could be considered, by those indifferent to its accomplishment as a goal in itself, as nevertheless an effective political instrument for achieving other, but related, goals. It was the latter aspect of woman suffrage that gave it its especial significance in the West, where the social ethic of woman suffrage conveniently corresponded to the broader social ethic of progressivism itself. Woman suffrage was, like the direct primary, the direct election of the Senate, the initiative, the referendum, and the recall, not only a reform in itself but an instrument for further reform within the prevailing political conception of social goals.

We may consider, for example, the parallel instance of the adoption of the initiative, the referendum, and the recall (along with woman suffrage) in California in 1911. These measures of popular democracy drew support from many quarters, as in their enactment various groups saw the means of furthering their own particular goals. According to V. O. Key, Jr. and Winston W. Crouch in *The Initiative and Referendum in California,* the movement for direct legislation had the support of such diverse groups as labor and farmer organizations, some business and commercial groups, the prohibition forces, the Socialist party, and local reform leagues.[1] As part of the prohibitionists' strategy in support of direct democracy, one county superintendent of the Anti-Saloon League counseled: "Perhaps Anti-Saloon Leagues, as such, should not come out in the open but they should be in the ranks, urging all kindred organizations to take an official stand for the measure."[2] The major thrust of this movement for direct democracy in California was directed at the power of a corrupt political machine which was, in turn, the servant of the Southern Pacific Railroad. Yet it is revealing to see the interlocking relationships involved in the impetus toward reform. In May 1907, a committee of reform-minded editors and lawyers met in Los Angeles and drafted a three-point action program. "The policies decided upon at the first meeting were: (1) to break the political control of the Southern Pacific; (2) to secure gradually the adoption of certain legislation which was considered to be fundamental, namely (a) the direct primary and (b) the initiative, the referendum, and the recall; and (3) to secure woman suffrage." [3] In 1910 the Progressive forces put through the direct primary in California and elected Hiram Johnson governor. In a special election the following year, some 23 constitutional amendments were voted upon, with all but one passing. The direct-legislation amendment passed overwhelmingly, with 168,744 for, 52,093 against.[4] Woman suffrage, however, just squeaked by, with 125,037 for, 121,450 against.[5]

This association of the initiative, the referendum, and the recall with woman suffrage may be seen further when we note that of the eleven states which had woman suffrage by the end of 1914, nine also had the initiative and referendum; while of the eleven states which had adopted the recall by this date, eight were also woman suffrage states.[6] The adoption of woman suffrage, however, generally ran behind that of direct legislation. For example, as early as 1902, Oregon adopted the initiative and referendum, yet woman suffrage was defeated there in 1900, 1906, and again in 1908, the year when the recall was adopted.

Clearly, the success of woman suffrage in the western states was due to its association in that region with the Progressive movement, which was bringing a new vitality to political reform forces during the years 1910–14. This made the woman suffrage movement a contributory part to a larger reform movement that was taking place in American politics. And it was this aspect of its relationship to the Progressive movement that made its associated goals significant. During the Progressive period the woman suffrage movement shared three social goals with the Progressives which made its own particular end, the enfranchisement of women, politically acceptable in the West. Goals is perhaps too limited a term to express the values, the status striving that permeate so much of the writing of woman suffrage advocates. Yet, recognizing the actual existence of some measure of imprecision, it nevertheless appears that the advocates of woman suffrage believed together with others in the Progressive movement in: the superiority of native-born, white Americans; the superiority of Protestant, indeed Puritan, morality; and the superiority of a kind of populism, of some degree of direct control over the state and city machines which, it was alleged, were dominated by the "interests." In this last point, there was, of course, a similarity to the Protestant Reformation itself with its intended search for a more direct relation between man and the Authority. Politically, this conjunction contributed to the overlap of the issues of woman suffrage with the direct primary, the initiative, the referendum, the recall, and the direct election of U.S. senators.

While woman suffrage resulted in a greater measure of equality in some sociopolitical relationships, it should not be overlooked that this benign result was often the by-product of a struggle for control by opposing forces committed to rather inequalitarian social goals. What may generally be defined as woman suffrage supporters consisted mostly of white, middle-class Protestants who were in the main native-born and who sought a purification, according to their lights, of the social and political order. Ultimately, this purification would include the economic order as well, dealing with such issues as child labor, the working condi-

tions of women in industry, and the range of economic opportunity for women. But initially, at least, these were
subordinate issues, and the acknowledgments of support
from trade unions, for example, in the official suffrage literature were so brief as to be nearly ungrateful when compared with the acknowledgments of support from the min-
istry, the womens' clubs, and the W.C.T.U. In this noneconomic aspect the struggle for woman suffrage and its
correlative values conforms to the pattern for the period
which Richard Hofstadter has succinctly labeled "status
politics." Many of those who led the Progressive movement
toward reform "were Progressives not because of economic
deprivations but primarily because they were victims of an
upheaval in status that took place in the United States during the closing decades of the nineteenth and the early years
of the twentieth century. Progressivism, in short, was to a
very considerable extent led by men who suffered from the
events of their time not through a shrinkage in their
means but through the changed pattern in the distribution
of deference and power." [7]

Among the most active supporters of woman suffrage
were ministers of the various Protestant denominations, in
particular the Methodists. Yet the clergy were, to turn
again to Hofstadter, "probably the most conspicuous losers
from the status revolution. . . . The increasingly vigorous interest in the social gospel, so clearly manifested by
the clergy after 1890, was in many respects an attempt to
restore through secular leadership some of the spiritual influence and authority and social prestige that clergymen
had lost through the upheaval in the system of status and
the secularization of society." [8] The truly remarkable economic and demographic changes that were transforming
America, so largely due to the spread of communications

and the increasing ease of transportation, were uprooting the old social system with its traditional lines of deference. As the early Protestant reformers sought to purify their religion by returning to primitive Christianity, so now did many of their descendants seek to purify America by curbing the new system of values if not reinstating the old. Woman suffrage could be seen as a device to achieve this end. The conspicuous evils of the present, now documented by the reporting of the muckrakers, could be contrasted with the purity of the past, and the purity possible in the future if men would choose wisely. George Mowry has observed: "This firm belief of the progressive in man's choice of ways helps to explain the evangelical character of the movement, the constant stress on 'the good man,' the 'moral position,' 'the right action.' Perhaps no other American political movement had such a righteous tone about it. It was, as Elmer Davis has said, a political 'carnival of purity.' " [9] The movement for woman suffrage was, to be sure, part of a movement for equal rights for women; but it would be a mistake to interpret the latter as simply making available to women the opportunities open to men. For, as Mowry noted,

> After seeing the manmade world at first-hand with its slums, dives, crooked politics, and almost ubiquitous double standards, many women naturally accepted the belief that their sex alone was the guardian of "the sacred vessels that held the ancient sanctities of life." . . . What they wanted was equality, but an equality based upon a standard of feminine virtue instead of masculine sin.[10]

*

There were many reasons for Americans to feel a sense of disenchantment, of resentment, of indignation about the established order in the opening decade of the twentieth century, for all that it was, in general, a time of economic prosperity. Various studies of the distribution of wealth at the time point to the conclusion that "fully eighty per cent of the people lived on the margin of existence while the wealth of the nation was owned by the remaining twenty per cent." [11] Yet even without any measurable degree of economic deprivation, there was a certain sense of disturbance that permeated much of the socially conscious literature of this era. Native-born Americans of every political outlook had a sharp sense of awareness that the older, traditional America was passing away, and that the newer America was not fulfilling the expectations of its founding fathers.

In part, this sense of resentment was a reaction to the conspicuous changes in America which had taken place after the Civil War. Industrialization, together with the extensive railroad system, had produced the sprawling metropolises which daily attracted young people from neighboring farms and from foreign lands. Urbanization made possible a new style of politics, as it made possible a new mode of life at every economic level, from the sordid slums of the tenement ghettos to the magnificent homes of the ostentatious rich. Both the splendor and the squalor were offensive to the middle class, which previously had not known either. An appeal for woman suffrage could be seen, in part, as an appeal for the standards of decency and righteousness that had prevailed at home; an appeal to the platitudes, the commonplaces, the little moral aphorisms which had been voiced in the kitchen or at the family table. In a sense, these provided the standard of justice for this secular reformation; these convictions of righteousness were, in a very basic sense, what the Progressive movement was all about.

In this sense of righteous indignation the woman suffragists of the Progressive movement were reliving the response of their Populist predecessors who had first felt the radical change in style of life that had taken place in America. Theirs was not, it should be noted, the response of a dwindling and isolated minority crying out against oppression at the hands of a hostile and tyrannical majority. It was, rather, the response of a majority who, certain of their numerical strength and righteousness of cause, believed they were losing power to a highly organized minority because of the ignorance and apathy and falling from grace of their fellow man. Only with this conviction could they seek to restore majority rule as the guiding instrument in politics. Progressive rallies seemed to some observors akin to revival meetings, for they were filled with evangelical zeal. The common enemy, to both secular and devout, was the corrupt political machine, supported by big business, pandering to vice, and enlisting in its ranks the voting cadres of ignorant foreigners. Sodom and Gomorrah were seen again in San Francisco, Portland, and Seattle; and the visible hosts of the opposition were the newly arrived immigrants. "Anglo-Saxons, whether Populist or patrician," Hofstadter has noted, "found it difficult to accept other peoples on terms of equality or trust." [12]

In the opening years of the twentieth century the issue of immigration had reached a crisis, and social reformers as diverse as J. Allen Smith, Jack London, and E. A. Ross were articulating themes of racial superiority and advocating immigration restriction. "The progressives, of course, had no monopoly on this racism," Mowry has observed. "But for one reason or another neither conservative nor radical was as vocal or as specific in his racism as was the reformer." [13] Woman suffrage, by the very nature of its nativist appeal, with its continued reminders that native-

born American women outnumbered foreign-born men
and women not only drew support from nativist Progressives but gave support to nativist goals.

Immigration had, of course, greatly contributed to the
urbanization that was taking place in the opening years of
the twentieth century. Over one million immigrants a year
entered the United States in 1905, 1906, 1907, 1910, 1913,
and 1914; by the latter year, approximately one third of
the population was composed of immigrants or the children of immigrants. Many of the foreign-born moved into
cities where some semblance of their native culture could
still be found. Lonely, gullible, often illiterate, and ignorant of the country and its ways, these "new" immigrants—distinguished from the "old" immigrants of northwestern Europe, England, and Ireland—were as much a
prey to boss politics as they were in need of boss services.
The confrontation of the new immigrant with the native
American produced something like a cultural shock; the
response it provoked helped give rise to Anthony Comstock and blue-stocking morality, and to an anxious concern about racial purity. The corruption in cities could be
seen in part as a product of the "new" immigration. And
at a time when many Americans were concerned about the
declining birth rate of the older immigrant stock, the high
birth rate of the new immigrants brought special concern
to those who had become caught up in the study of eugenics early in the twentieth century. Writing of the eugenics
movement, John Higham observed:

> Its emphasis on unalterable human inequalities con-
> firmed the patricians' sense of superiority; its warnings
> over the multiplication of the unfit and the sterility of the
> best people synchronized with the discussion of race sui-
> cide. Yet the eugenicists' dedication to a positive program

of "race improvement" through education and state
action gave the movement an air of reform, enabling it to
attract the support of many progressives while still minis-
tering to conservative sensibilities. By 1910, therefore,
eugenicists were catching the public ear. From then
through 1914, according to one tabulation, the general
magazines carried more articles on eugenics than on the
three questions of slums, tenements, and living standards,
combined.[14]

The growing concern with eugenics, together with the
new immigration, focused attention on a cleavage in the
American political community between the old stock and
the new, and gave rise to the claim that "pure" old stock
was somehow synonymous with "pure" political morality.
The stuggle against corruption blended easily into a kind
of xenophobia in which virtue and morality were called
upon to triumph over the immigrant power supposedly
controlled by the bosses and the interests. On the West
Coast this conflict was aggravated by the presence of a relatively small number of Asiatics. In 1890, after Chinese immigration had been cut off, there were nearly 107,000 Chinese in America; by 1910, this number had been reduced
to approximately half that amount. Japanese immigrants,
however, who had numbered approximately 2000 in 1890,
totaled over 67,000 in 1910, most of whom settled in California. This influx had been terminated in 1907 by the so-
called "Gentleman's Agreement." [15] In 1910, California
had a total population of over 2,250,000; yet many white
Californians protested that they were being inundated by a
"yellow peril," and began likening their situation to that
of white Southerners who also, it was asserted, lived with
an unassimilable race.

In many respects, the West and the South followed a

similar course on the immigration issue. As had been evident in the days of populism, the South and the West possessed many similarities in political outlook. Both regions were predominantly populated by native-born Americans; in the days of the old immigration both regions had sought to attract immigrant settlers; now, early in the twentieth century, both regions favored immigration restriction, in spite of the fact that "the whole area beyond the Rockies and below the Mason and Dixon Line had only half as many new immigrants as did New York City." [16]

Along with the new immigration into the eastern and midwestern cities, an internal migration of considerable proportion took place. In large measure, this was composed of native-born Americans moving, once again, westward. In 1887, a migration of major proportions funneled into Los Angeles; it was called the "Pullman migration" after its railroad sponsorship. This movement was, fundamentally, a Protestant one, and it not only changed the religious basis of power in southern California but left its mark on subsequent California history. "The Protestant migration," Gilman Ostrander has noted, "was from the first directed to the unpopulated lands of southern California, and with the boom of 1887 the dominant culture of that land became the culture of rural, Protestant, native, temperance-minded America." [17] For decades the population of Los Angeles, reflecting this and subsequent migrations, doubled with each census: it reached 50,000 in 1890; over 100,000 in 1900; over 300,000 in 1910; nearly 600,000 in 1920 (thus exceeding San Francisco's). During the decade of 1900–10 a sharp increase took place in the number of the new foreign-born immigrants into the South and West; however, the percentage of new immigrants was still astonishingly small to have provoked such a furor of opposition from the restrictionists. "In 1910 the new immigration constituted 1 per cent of the white population in the South and 5.6 per cent in the Pacific states." [18] It would seem evident that nativism thrived most successfully in those regions in which the presence of foreign-born settlers was least significant politically. Equally evident was the fact that the presence of Asiatics on the West Coast provoked the same racist response which had long been associated with the views of many white Southerners about the presence of Negroes in the South. The two regions, the South and the West, combined to lead an assault upon the existing immigration system at the very height of the Progressive movement. John Higham suggests a further explanation for the timing of this response:

> If we conclude that the penetration of the new immigration into the South and West automatically activated the color phobias of those areas, we do little justice to the distinctive essence of all nativisms. In every guise, the nativist stood always as a nationalist in a defensive posture. He chose a *foreign* adversary, and defined him, in terms of a conception of the nation's most precious and precarious attributes. Along with the social impact of the new immigration, the South and the Far West in the early twentieth century were also tingling with the ideological stimulus of a new nationalism. Perhaps the kind of nationalism that flourished in the wake of the Spanish-American War did as much as anything else to enable the guardians of white supremacy to discharge their feelings on the new foreign groups.[19]

Yet it must not be forgotten that in the West, as in the South, a belief in white supremacy had been embedded in its culture, its laws, and its daily life. As C. Vann Woodward has observed, at the time that slavery existed in the

South, the West offered no refuge of freedom and equality. "Generally speaking, the farther west the Negro went in the free states the harsher he found the proscription and segregation." [20] In the Oregon constitution of 1857, free Negroes and mulattoes were henceforth prohibited from entering the state.[21] Both Oregon and California failed to ratify the Fifteenth Amendment.

We may now return to the query posed in the first chapter of this study: Was there more than coincidence to the fact that Negro suffrage was proscribed in the South at the time that woman suffrage arose in the West? The answer is yes. In both regions native-born white Americans sought to maintain a supremacy in politics commensurate with their presumed superiority in the social system. In the West, woman suffrage contributed to this end by increasing the number of native-born white voters; in the South this goal was accomplished by restricting the franchise of nonwhite Americans through use of the grandfather's clause, the poll tax and the white primary. In both intances the altering of the franchise accorded with the nativist sentiment that was such a significant part of the political perspective of the South and West during the Progressive era. In the West, the extension of woman suffrage conformed in many respects to the pattern set in Utah in the days of the Mormon conflict with the "gentiles"; for in the entire West, as earlier in Utah, woman suffrage made an effective political instrument to preserve a social ethic in response to the immigration of those perceived to be outsiders.

*

In 1885, in a book evidently designed for Protestants and significantly titled *Our Country*, the Reverend Josiah

Strong, a supporter of woman suffrage, wrote that the evils facing the country could be summed up under the headings of Romanism, Mormonism, Immigration, Socialism, Urbanization, and Intemperance. The Anglo-Saxons, Strong argued, had brought to mankind the great contributions of civil liberty and spiritual Christianity. And, he enquired, "Is there room for reasonable doubt that this race, unless devitalized by alcohol and tobacco, is destined to dispossess many weaker races, assimilate others, and mold the remainder, until, in a very true and important sense, it has Anglo-Saxonized mankind?" [22] The importance of a prohibition on the consumption, sale or manufacture of alcoholic beverages throughout the land was basic to the beliefs of many Anglo-Saxonizers. And probably no other attempted reform of the Progressive era was so distinctively Protestant in terms of its late nineteenth- and early twentieth-century supporters. In the nineteenth century, a taboo against the consumption of alcohol, particularly of hard liquor, came increasingly to serve as a Protestant article of faith and became as characteristic of many Protestant sects as the proscribing of pork was for Jews, or the proscribing of meat on Fridays was for Catholics. This was as true of the recent religions of American origin, such as the Church of the Latter-day Saints, and Christian Science, as it was of older Protestant faiths: Quaker, Methodist, Baptist, Congregational, and Presbyterian. Episcopalians were apparently divided on the issue, as were Lutherans; "The older English-speaking Lutherans and the Swedish Lutherans of the Augustana Synod were most strongly evangelical and the most devoted to temperance reform." [23] In a recent study of prohibition during the Progressive era, James H. Timberlake found that: "The American religious community, . . . compris-

ing about 40 per cent of the total population, was divided
over prohibition. On the one side were most Protestants,
led by the Presbyterian, Methodist, Baptist, and Congregational churches; on the other side were most Roman Catholics and Jews." [24] In fact, critics of the Anti-Saloon
League asserted that the prohibition movement was only a
disguise on the part of those seeking "Protestant political
supremacy." [25]

As might be expected, given the heavy Protestant migration to California, Los Angeles County became a major
source of strength for both prohibition and the woman
suffrage movement. In 1896 and in 1911, Los Angeles
voted in favor of woman suffrage contrary to the period's
usual pattern of urban opposition. (San Francisco voted
against woman suffrage in both elections.)

Prohibition, like woman suffrage, brought support to
the Progressive movement and drew support from it; yet
there seems little doubt that the prime advocate of prohibition was the Protestant, native American. In California,
for example, prohibition gained political significance
whenever nativism rose up to new heights.[26] The Prohibitionists in turn brought support to such Progressive measures as "woman suffrage, initiative, referendum, and recall, and bills designed to suppress gambling and prostitution." [27] Because the main strength of the prohibitionists
came from "the old-stock, middle-class section of the
American community," which was predominant in the
countryside, the issue, like woman suffrage, tended to appear as a conflict between rural and urban America. Yet, as
Timberlake has noted, "The essential fact about the prohibition movement is not that it was either rural or urban,
but that it was a middle-class reform that won the support
of middle-class Protestants in both country and city." [28]

From the beginnings of the nineteenth-century temperance movement it had been associated with the cause of woman suffrage. After the Civil War, woman suffrage had become a repeated plank in the Prohibition party platform. Some of the most familiar names in woman suffrage history—Susan B. Anthony, Carrie Chapman Catt, Anna Howard Shaw—came into the movement through the temperance issue.[29] And no organization mentioned in the massive six-volume *History of Woman Suffrage* could vie with the W.C.T.U. in favorable, grateful references. In fact, the support of woman suffrage by the Prohibitionists sometimes created political problems for the former movement, for it confirmed the suspicion of the "wets" that woman suffrage would bring about prohibition. In Oregon, before the 1906 election on woman suffrage, the Brewers' and Wholesale Liquor Dealers' Association sent to its customers a secret circular containing the following message:

> Dear Sir:—Two laws are to be voted on at the election June 4, which are of vital importance to every liquor merchant in Oregon without exception. The first is woman suffrage. The second is the amendment to the local option law. The members of this association have worked hard for a long time on both these matters . . . but, being few in number, they can not by themselves pass the local option amendment or defeat woman suffrage. That part of the work is up to the retailers. We write this letter earnestly to ask you to help.[30]

In 1912, Oregon adopted woman suffrage; two years later it adopted prohibition. In 1910, it was arranged in advance of the suffrage referendum in the state of Washington that "in order not to antagonize the 'whiskey' vote, the temper-

ance women would submerge their hard-earned honors
and let the work of their unions go unheralded." [31]
Woman suffrage won, and prohibition came to Washington four years later. Between 1914 and 1917, seven western
states adopted prohibition; all of them were woman
suffrage states. [32]

There were many reasons why prohibition was seen as
an important aspect of the Progressive movement. "As an
integral part of the Progressive Movement," Timberlake
has noted, "prohibition drew on the same moral idealism
and sought to deal with the same basic problems. If the
Progressive Movement was nourished on a belief in the
moral law, so was prohibition, which sought to remove
from commerce an article that was believed to despoil
man's reason and undermine the foundation of religion
and representative government." [33] Yet it must not be forgotten that prohibition represented a kind of social control
exercised by one portion of the community over the rest.
At the beginning of the twentieth century, five states had
statewide prohibition: Maine, Kansas, North Dakota, New
Hampshire, and Vermont. (The latter two returned to
local option in 1903.) But the subsequent course of the
prohibition movement reveals a very significant pattern,
for it followed the path of nativist strength. Prohibition, of
one form or another, had been a method of social control
ever since liquor, along with firearms, had been forbidden
to the Indians; it was but a logical extension of this belief
that caused liquor to be denied to Negroes in the South.
The southern states, where the percentage of native-born
Americans was highest (approximately 97.5 in 1910),
formed the first section to adopt prohibition on a broad
scale. Between 1907 and 1915, Georgia, Alabama, Mississippi, North Carolina, West Virginia, Virginia, Arkansas,

and South Carolina adopted prohibition; this was also the period in which the disfranchisement of Negroes was completed. The prohibition victories next occurred in the northcentral, Rocky Mountain, and far western states where the percentage of native-born (about 82) was not as high as in the South but higher than in the remaining eastern sector (about 76). Between 1914 and 1917, prohibition was adopted in Washington, Oregon, Colorado, Arizona, Idaho, Montana, Utah, Iowa, South Dakota, Nebraska, Michigan, and Indiana.[34] The implication that the standards of morality subscribed to by native-born Americans were the only legitimate ones obviously created difficulties for the woman suffrage movement, so intertwined was it with the prohibition movement. In particular, offense was given to many Germans for whom successful brewing marked a distinctive cultural accomplishment and who were, for the most part either Catholic or non-Prohibitionist Lutherans. For example, in the unsuccessful woman suffrage election in Nebraska in November 1914, the state German-American Alliance sent out the following appeal, written in German:

> We consider the proposed amendment to the constitution granting the right of suffrage to women as the most important question which will be decided at the coming election. Our State Alliance took a most decided stand against woman suffrage at its annual convention. . . . Our German women do not want the right to vote, and since our opponents desire the right of suffrage mainly for the purpose of saddling the yoke of prohibition on our necks, we should oppose it with all our might. . . . We most earnestly urge our friends of German speech and German descent not to permit business or other consid-

erations to prevent them from going to the polls and cast-
ing their ballots as above directed.[35]

In Ohio, in 1912, the official *History of Woman Suffrage*
reported that, "The German-American Alliance and the
Personal Liberty League, two associations representing the
brewers' interests, fought it in the field as they had done
in the convention." [36] In North Dakota, in 1913, the report was much the same: "The chief opponents were the
German Russians in Emmons and surrounding counties. . . ." [37]

In an analysis of the election of 1911 which brought
woman suffrage to California, one writer noted that while
a leading rabbi favored woman suffrage, the Jewish vote
went against it. It will be recalled that Catholics and Jews
were also generally on the antiprohibition side. While the
Catholic vote had been opposed in 1896, in the second
election many priests supported it and, "The suffragists
undoubtedly polled a fair proportion of Catholic votes this
time." However, this suffragette's report continued:

The Germans were generally opposed even when they
were Socialists. The lower class Italians were all opposed,
though the leading Italian papers had indorsed the measure. Doctors as a class were opposed, particularly those
who had fought the entrance of women into the medical
profession every step of the way. It is astonishing how
men can endure to see women breaking their backs at
janitress's work or at the wash tub without a thought of
their overworking or leaving the home sphere, but are
worried to death as soon as a woman earns an income of
$5,000 a year in the medical profession and begins to
drive about in her own automobile. Lawyers as a class
were in favor of suffrage. . . . Protestant clergymen and

university professors and teachers were generally for suffrage.

And in a peroration which rather sums up the ethic of this Puritan, middle-class, native American, feminine reformation, the author recounted the long procession of suffrage forces on election day:

> It looked as if the whole world were going to a funeral. And it was a funeral—a funeral for the corrupt and special interests; a funeral for the dive and the white slaver and the low saloon, which is a feeder for these. For the men were not traveling those distances to put a cross against "No" of amendment four. They were voting to take the wife who had pioneered, who had crossed the plains or lived uncomplainingly where neighbors were few, who had been a hewer of wood and drawer of water —they were voting to take that wife or a schoolteaching daughter or a wise old mother out of the class with lunatics and criminals and put her on a footing with other intelligent human beings. . . . More than the course of empire takes its way westward. Liberty for *all* the people is coming out of the West.[38]

In sum, it may be said that the woman suffrage movement triumphed in the West during the Progressive era because it was aided by, even as it contributed to, the Progressive triumphs there. Had woman suffrage stood alone as an issue in itself doubtless it would have been defeated again as it had been in many of these states in the past. But as part of a broader movement which was seeking to arrogate political power to native-born white Americans, it was able to capitalize on the course of this general movement. Political equality for women in the western states can be seen, therefore, as a by-product of the western Puritan revival.

CHAPTER VI

Eve of Reform

Woman will raise the standard in politics as she has
raised and maintained the standard in every relation
she sustains in life.

Representative Philip P. Campbell (R-Kans.)

The movement toward a Puritan revival in America, coming out of the West on the eve of World War I, contained numerous intended reforms which could be reduced to a single underlying goal: to purify American politics. The initiative, the referendum, and the recall, the direct primary, the direct election of the Senate, woman
suffrage, prohibition, and immigration restriction—all
were attempts to change the political rules of the game
that may best be understood within the context of the
proposition that political power had fallen into the hands
of the corrupted or the corruptible and needed to be restored to the people. To purify politics required the re-
moval of the political intermediaries, the party bosses, who
stood between the ballot box and public policy. Yet behind the issue of whether the bosses or the people should
rule America lurked the subtler question: which people?

Women, it was generally assumed, were more moral
than men and would therefore as voters contribute to the
purification of politics. Prohibition, it was thought, was
simply the everyday practice of the restriction on selling

liquor during elections which already existed in many states. The literacy test for immigration would check the flow of illiterate, and presumably corruptible, immigrants into the nation. If the effect of woman suffrage would be to change the political electorate, the effect of restrictive immigration would be to limit the political base to native-born Americans and immigrants from England, Ireland, and northwest Europe. Because this political reformation was fundamentally white, Anglo-Saxon, and Protestant in its underlying ethos, at no stage in its development was it seriously proposed that the restrictive white primary in the South was in any way improper. Status reform, more than economic reform, was the issue. For all the talk about democracy and equality which accompanied the woman suffrage movement in the West, the general tendency of the reformation of which it was a part was not so much to broaden the base of political power as to change its locus. This may be seen by noting the close relationship in the West of woman suffrage, prohibition, and immigration restriction, and then by comparing this relationship with that found in the South and East on these three issues.

We may now corroborate the rhetoric of these associated reforms with Congressional voting data on them. This corroboration is facilitated by the fact that the 63rd Congress, elected in 1912, voted on all three of these issues. We have a record, therefore, of how the same representatives at virtually the same point of time decided the relative worth or political significance of each of these issues. There is an additional advantage in utilizing the vote of the 63rd Congress for analysis, because this was the first Congress to vote in both houses on woman suffrage. Although what became the Nineteenth Amendment was voted on by three Congresses, the 63rd, 65th, and 66th, before it acquired the necessary two-thirds vote of both houses to become a proposed amendment, in the 63rd Congress we may see the first national test of the issue. Ultimately, as we shall see, the western ethos prevailed.

*

In the United States Senate the woman suffrage amendment first came to a vote on January 25, 1887, at which time it was defeated by a vote of 16 ayes to 34 nays, with 26 not voting. All 16 ayes came from Republicans; 11 Republicans contributed to the nays. The issue was not voted upon in the Senate again until March 19, 1914 (the 63rd Congress); then it barely passed with 35 ayes to 34 nays, lacking of course the necessary two thirds. Of the 35 ayes, 20 were Republicans, 14 were Democrats, and one was Progressive. Of the 34 nays, 22 were Democrats and 12 were Republicans. (Sixteen Democrats and ten Republicans did not vote.) While the Senate vote shows the Republicans to be more sympathetic to woman suffrage than were the Democrats, it also reveals a regional pattern of voting on the issue. If we drop a line south along the western shore of Lake Michigan, down the eastern border of Illinois, and then west across the northern borders of Arkansas and Texas, we enclose 21 states, which for purposes of this analysis we will call West. These states recorded a Senate vote in favor of the woman suffrage amendment of 27 ayes to 6 nays. The 27 states east and south of this line record a Senate vote opposing woman suffrage by an almost identical margin of 8 ayes to 28 nays. We must now divide the South from the East by separating out the 11 former states of the Confederacy and calling the states north of Tennessee and Virginia, and east of Illinois, East. In Table II the Senate vote of 1914 on the woman suffrage amendment is presented in terms of this regional breakdown.[1]

TABLE II

SENATE VOTE ON WOMAN SUFFRAGE BY REGIONS, 63RD CONGRESS

	Western States	Southern States	Eastern States	Total
Ayes	27	3	5	35
Nays	6	13	15	34

On January 12, 1915, the House voted on the woman suffrage amendment. It was defeated by a vote of 174 ayes to 204 nays. The ayes were made up of 88 Democrats and 86 Republicans and Progressives; the nays were made up of 173 Democrats and 31 Republicans. In Table III the House vote is distributed according to regions.[2]

TABLE III

HOUSE VOTE ON WOMAN SUFFRAGE BY REGIONS, 63RD CONGRESS

	West	South	East	Total
Ayes	95	7	72	174
Nays	28	98	78	204
Not voting	12	10	31	53
Total	135	115	181	431

It now becomes readily apparent that the main support for woman suffrage came out of the West; the South was overwhelmingly opposed to the issue, while the East was nearly evenly divided. It is also evident that much of the Democratic opposition to woman suffrage came out of the one-party South. No southern state recorded a majority favora-

ble to woman suffrage. In the West, only Nebraska (1–4)
and Wisconsin (2–9) recorded a majority opposed to
woman suffrage; in the East, woman suffrage received a
favorable majority in Massachusetts (8–6), Michigan (9–2),
New Jersey (7–4), Pennsylvania (20–9), and West Virgiana
(4–1).

*

In the West, 95 congressmen voted for the amendment,
while 28 opposed it; in addition, 12 were listed as not voting. Political party distribution does not appear to be particularly significant in this vote. Of the 68 western Democrats, 47, or approximately 69 per cent, voted favorably on
the issue; of the 56 Republicans, 39, or approximately 70
per cent, did the same; the 11 Progressives and Independ-
ents gave 9, or nearly 82 per cent to woman suffrage.

The distribution of votes according to clearly rural and
clearly urban districts also did not make a significant
difference in the West. By the time this vote was taken,
statewide woman suffrage existed in eleven western states
and, since 1913, women had been permitted to vote in
Illinois for presidential electors. Of the 73 clearly rural
representatives, 53, or nearly 73 per cent, voted for woman
suffrage; of the 30 clearly urban representatives, 20, or
nearly 67 per cent, voted for the amendment. These results
in the West are summarized in Table IV.

However woman suffrage received a clear mandate from
the representatives of that broad expanse of continent which
reached from eastern Illinois to the Pacific Coast. States
which, themselves, could not enact woman suffrage by
popular referendum could, nevertheless, because of their
districting, elect representatives of whom a majority were
favorable to woman suffrage. Of the 21 western states, only

TABLE IV

VOTE OF WESTERN REPRESENTATIVES ON WOMAN
SUFFRAGE AMENDMENT, 63RD CONGRESS

	Demo-crats		Republi-cans		Progres-sives		Rural		Urban		Total	
Ayes	47	69%	39	70%	9	82%	53	73%	20	67%	95	70%
Nays	17	25%	11	20%	0	0%	14	19%	9	30%	28	21%
Not voting	4	6%	6	10%	2	18%	6	8%	9	3%	12	9%
Total	68	100%	56	100%	11	100%	73	100%	30	100%	135	100%

11 had statewide woman suffrage by the time this vote was taken; yet eight of the remaining ten states strongly supported the measure. Furthermore, as we have seen, neither political party nor the rural or urban character of the district proved to be a very discriminative factor in the West.

*

When we shift our focus to the South, we see quite readily how the issue of white supremacy dominated all other political considerations. Yet we must remember that the doctrine of white supremacy was not confined to the South alone in 1914. Aileen S. Kraditor, in *The Ideas of the Woman Suffrage Movement, 1890–1920,* has observed: "The development of the woman suffrage organization from a strictly Northern group of crusaders for the rights of all men and women to a nationwide association that all but officially sanctioned second-class citizenship for Negroes may be traced in specific events in the history of the NAWSA [National American Woman Suffrage Association]." [3] Doubtless, the acquiescence by the official woman suffrage organization in the denial of Negro voting rights in the South reflected a wish to conciliate Southerners at a time when the woman suffrage forces needed all the support they could get. Yet, as has been indicated earlier, there was a considerable amount of nativism in the woman suffrage movement, and racism was the handmaiden of nativism. The belief in white supremacy and indeed nativism, which was so much a part of the overt politics of the South, was present, although more covertly so, and to a lesser degree, in much of the rest of the country in 1914. It was implicit in the charges made by Carrie Chapman Catt and Nettie Shuler that woman suffrage referendums were defeated in the West because the United States Brewers' Association had "organized the Russian vote against woman suffrage in the Dakotas, the German vote in Nebraska, Missouri and Iowa, the Negro vote in Kansas and Oklahoma, the Chinese vote in California." [4] Racism was also evident in the speeches of some of the opponents of the woman suffrage amendment such as Senator Borah (R-Ida.), who spoke in the Senate as follows:

> Mr. President, we are not a homogeneous people yet by any means. We have the Oriental question on the Pacific slope, we have the Negro question in the South, and we have the countless thousands of immigrants crowding to this country from Southern Europe, who are yet to become acquainted with our theory of citizenship. . . . There are 10,000 Japanese and Chinese women in . . . [the Pacific slope] states, and I have no particular desire to bestow suffrage upon them; I have not any desire to yield up to them a voice in deciding the question how we shall control our schools on the Pacific slope.[5]

This view was supported by Senator Pittman (D-Nev.), who declared that while he favored woman suffrage, he could not endorse a federal amendment as the means of its accomplishment. "We are facing," he stated, "just as serious problems as to what our relations shall be toward the

Japanese and Chinese as the people of the South are with regard to the Negroes." [6] His colleague, Senator Newlands (D-Nev.), who voted for the amendment, sought to restrict suffrage in terms of race rather than sex, believing "that this country is subject to greater menace from the race question than any other. . . ." Further, he continued, "No reasoning can satisfy my mind that it is right to exclude the white woman from the electorate of this country. I stand, therefore, for the extension of suffrage to white women. I stand for the denial of the right of suffrage in this country to the people of any other race than the white race." [7] In the vote on an amendment to the woman suffrage proposal which would have restricted the franchise to "white citizens," the only nonsouthern votes recorded for it were those of Senator Myers (D-Mont.) and the two senators from Nevada.

The racism latent in the West, where the whites were clearly in the majority, was made manifest in the South, where the ratio between the races was much closer. Southerners feared that the woman suffrage amendment would produce two results, both opposed by the white supremacists: (1) it would endorse the principle of federal authority over the suffrage, already present in the Fifteenth Amendment, and (2) it would grant the franchise to Negro women. On the floor of the Senate, Mississippi Senators Vardaman and Williams presented a blatant racist doctrine, and they sought amendments to the proposed suffrage amendment which would ultimately achieve, in the words of Senator Vardaman, "the repeal of the fifteenth, the modification of the fourteenth Amendment . . . making this Government a government by white men, of white men, for all men, which will be but the re-

alization of the dream of the founders of the Republic." [8]
Senator Williams declared that "The fifteenth amendment
was a horrible blunder and a horrible mistake. . . . That
amendment created race feeling in this country that never
existed prior to it." [9] Further, he stated, "I want this to be
a white man's country, governed by white men." [10] Issues
of race took precedence over issues of sex in the southern
discussion of the woman suffrage amendment, and the underlying ethos as evidenced in both voting and speeches
was the presumed superiority of the native-born white.

In the House, southern representatives sometimes
masked the racist issue with ornamental oratory. Thus Representative Clark (D-Fla.) declared:

> The Word of God inveighs against woman suffrage, and
> the plans of the Creator would be, in a measure, sub-
> verted by its adoption. . . . Are we ready to repudiate
> the Scriptures and supplant God's place with this scheme
> of dissatisfied women and office-seeking demagogues? . . .
> Let us, then, leave woman where she is—the loveliest of
> all creation, queen of the household, and undisputed dic-
> tator of the destiny of man.[11]

It was evident, however, that Representative Clark's re-
marks were restricted to white women, as were those of
Representative Webb (D-N.C.) when he observed: "I am
unwilling, as a southern man, to force upon her any bur-
den which will distract this loving potentate from her sacred, God-imposed duties." [12]

The overwhelming southern vote in the House against
the woman suffrage amendment (7 ayes, 98 nays) was in
effect a vote against a further extension of the franchise in
the South. Only three Southern Democrats joined with the
four southern Republicans to support the woman suffrage

amendment. It was, furthermore, a party vote, for 98 of
the 111 Democrats, or 89 per cent, in the House voted together.

*

When we shift our focus to the East, we find quite
different results from those we have seen in the other two
sections. In the first place, the 181 eastern votes were almost evenly divided on the woman suffrage amendment,
with 72 ayes and 78 nays. When we look at this vote from
the point of view of party identification, however, we no-
tice a real division on the issue. Of the 114 eastern Democrats, only 38, or 33 per cent of them, favored the issue;
while of the 57 eastern Republicans, some 26, or 46 per
cent, voted aye. Of the 10 Progressives in the East, 8 voted
for the woman suffrage amendment. When we look at the
character of the districts involved in the vote and separate
the clearly rural and the clearly urban, we find that the
rural districts were only slightly less opposed to woman
suffrage than the urban ones. Of the 93 eastern congressmen from rural areas, only 37, or about 40 per cent, favored the issue; of the 75 representatives from urban dis-

TABLE V

VOTE OF EASTERN REPRESENTATIVES ON WOMAN
SUFFRAGE AMENDMENT, JANUARY 12, 1915

	Demo-crats		Republi-cans		Progres-sives		Rural		Urban		Total
Ayes	38	33%	26	46%	8	80%	37	40%	26	35%	72
Nays	58	51%	20	35%	0	0%	40	43%	36	48%	78
Not voting	18	16%	11	19%	2	20%	16	17%	13	17%	31
Total	114	100%	57	100%	10	100%	93	100%	75	100%	181

tricts, only 26, or 35 per cent, supported woman suffrage. The results of this analysis are summarized in Table V.

In the East, by 1915, the woman suffrage movement, once composed largely of native American feminists and their prohibition allies, had found new support among trade unionists, social reformers, and socialists. In 1909, *Harper's Weekly* reported that the woman suffrage movement had gained more strength in one year in New York City than in the twenty preceding years. And *The New York Times,* which was then opposed to woman suffrage, noted that the trade unions had become "training schools for the woman-suffrage organizations." [13] As the woman suffrage movement developed in the northeastern states just prior to World War I, it attracted, in addition to labor unions, a host of other social reformers, people interested in abolishing child labor, in establishing maximum hours of work for women, and minimum rates of pay. In the Eastern states status politics mixed with the politics of economics. In these states, with their textile mills and garment sweatshops and high percentage of women employees, woman suffrage could be seen as an important instrument for achieving social reform legislation. As such, it was feared by economic conservatives. For example, the week before the House voted on the proposed suffrage amendment, Mrs. Arthur M. Dodge, president of the National Association Opposed to Woman Suffrage, announced that behind the woman suffrage movement was ". . . Socialism such as the American Republic repudiates, and is trying to hold in check. . . . Go out and emphasize to the business man, to the workingman this alliance between woman suffrage and Socialism; tell them that the Socialist vote would be nearly doubled through the extension of the ballot to women. . . ." [14] The evident concern, by 1914, with the possible political implications of a woman's vote caused Anna Howard Shaw, president of the National American Suffrage Association, to write:

> Many women feel that the greatest good they can do with the ballot is to abolish commercialized vice, to prevent child labor, or to make effective their protest against war. This is perhaps true. We all agree that these evils must be abolished, and that women, unenfranchised, have not been able to abolish them. But the evils themselves and the desire of women to right them do not constitute the reason women should be enfranchised. The reason would remain even though all the evils I have named, or could name should be abolished at once.[15]

In the East, supporters of woman suffrage were faced with the difficult task of trying to appeal to economic reformers without at the same time alienating social conservatives.

*

The thesis has been advanced in this book that the support behind the woman suffrage movement in the West was essentially Puritan in its underlying ethos and outlook. In the sense in which the term Puritan is used here, it does not signify a variation of Calvinism or even necessarily Protestantism; it signifies rather a way of looking at the world and the social relationships contained therein. It was heavily imbued with a moral commitment to right the wrongs of society and to check by law, where possible, the intrusion of evil. Many lasting reforms—the reduction of child labor, standards of health and safety for the employment of women, a new emphasis on education for women of all ages—came out of this Puritan revival in addition to

woman suffrage itself. Appropriately, the heir to the political legacy it created is the League of Women Voters.

Yet, as has been noted above, the woman suffrage movement, in the West in particular, became associated with
two supposed reforms of the time which were not so lasting: prohibition and restrictive immigration legislation.
While both of these issues had their economic aspects, they
may be seen fundamentally as issues of status in an America that was becoming rapidly transformed by immigration
and urbanization. As such they became closely related issues, for the question "whose morality?" led directly to the
question "whose power?"

Prohibition, like woman suffrage, came into its peak
years of support during the Progressive era. It was looked
upon by its supporters as a major social reform of a truly
progressive, civilized society. As Senator Gronna (R-N.D.)
remarked in support of the woman suffrage amendment:

> I believe that this Nation will soon, and that all nations
> must ultimately, stamp out the liquor curse, if they are
> not to perish from the earth. And I believe that giving the
> women the vote will hasten the day when this is accom-
> plished in the United States. I know that in my State the
> influence of the women is what made it possible to banish
> the saloon.[16]

By 1917, eight of the eleven western woman-suffrage
states were "dry" (Kansas, Washington, Oregon, Colorado,
Arizona, Idaho, Montana, Utah); in all, there was a total
of 26 dry states by April 1917.[17] In 1913 the dry forces
won a major victory, the enactment of the Webb-Kenyon
bill, over the veto of President Taft. The Webb-Kenyon
Act made it illegal to ship intoxicating liquors into any
state in violation of the laws of that state. In his analysis of

the Senate vote overriding President Taft's veto of the bill, James H. Timberlake noted that "The vote for the Webb-Kenyon bill came primarily from those areas where the old-stock middle classes were strongest." [18] Fortified by victory in 1913, the prohibition forces introduced the Hobson resolution, or prohibition amendment, into Congress the following year. It was this amendment which the 63rd Congress voted upon but three weeks before its vote on woman suffrage. In this Congress the prohibition amendment fared better than did the woman suffrage amendment, for on December 22, 1914, the House of Representatives passed the measure by a vote of 197 ayes, 190 nays. It failed to receive, of course, the two-thirds majority required for an amendment.

Joseph R. Gusfield in his analysis of prohibition as a status conflict, or to use his apt title, a "symbolic crusade," notes: "The Eighteenth Amendment was the high point of the struggle to assert the public dominance of old middle-class values. It established the victory of Protestant over Catholic, rural over urban, tradition over modernity, the middle class over both the lower and the upper strata." He finds, therefore, the significance of the issue "in the fact that it happened." Furthermore he observes:

> The establishment of Prohibition laws was a battle in the struggle for status between two divergent styles of life. It marked the public affirmation of the abstemious, ascetic qualities of American Protestantism. In this sense, it was an act of ceremonial deference toward old middle-class culture. If the law was often disobeyed and not enforced, the respectability of its adherents was honored in the breach. After all, it was *their* law that drinkers had to avoid.[19]

We have seen that the question of "whose America?" continually underlay the rhetoric of the woman suffrage movement, just as the question of "whose morality?" determined the course of the prohibition issue. Nor were these questions overlooked by the opponents of these measures. In an editorial against prohibition, the Catholic journal *America* noted the energetic activities of the W.C.T.U. and observed: "If public authority has the duty of aiding men and women to be temperate, it has also the duty of protecting the people at large against fanaticism." And in the week that the House voted on woman suffrage, an editorial in *America* stated: "Whatever may be said of the intrinsic merits of this question, the 'votes for women' movement is decidedly unfortunate in some of its feminine advocates, whose unchristian principles and methods fill Catholics with distrust and aversion." [20]

In Table VI the vote of the House of Representatives of the 63rd Congress on prohibition is presented, broken down into regions and placed beside the vote of these Representatives on woman suffrage.[21]

TABLE VI

VOTE COMPARISON ON WOMAN SUFFRAGE AND PROHIBITION
AMENDMENTS IN PERCENTAGES

[NOTE: Prohibition results are italicized.]

	West (N = 135) %	South (N = 115) %	East (N = 181) %	Woman Suffrage	Prohib.
Ayes	70 *57*	6 *61*	40 *28*	174	*197*
Nays	21 *35*	85 *29*	43 *60*	204	*190*
Not voting	9 *8*	9 *10*	17 *12*	53	*44*
				431	*431*

In the West, prohibition received the support of 39, or 57 per cent, of the Democrats, and 30, or 54 per cent, of the Republicans. Progressives gave 8 of their 11 votes, or 73 per cent, to prohibition. When we distinguish the clearly rural and clearly urban districts in the West, we find that prohibition ran nearly as well in the rural areas as woman suffrage, receiving 50 of a possible 73 votes, or about 69 per cent. In the urban areas, however, we find a decided break between prohibition and woman suffrage support. Out of a possible 30 urban votes, prohibition received only 8, or about 27 per cent; woman suffrage received 20 votes in these same districts, or some 67 per cent of the urban vote.

We may pass over the predominantly rural and one-party South, with its strong support of prohibition, to look at the more interesting vote in the East on this issue. There we find a significant party division on prohibition. The eastern Democrats gave only 14 out of a possible 114 votes, or 12 per cent, to prohibition; the eastern Republicans, on the other hand, gave 26 out of a possible 57 votes, or 46 per cent, to prohibition. However, congressmen of both parties from rural districts in the East gave 35 out of 93 votes, or 38 per cent to prohibition, while in the urban districts it attracted only 7 out of a possible 75 votes, or merely 9 per cent. A summary comparison of the voting on the Hobson prohibition amendment in the East and West is provided in Table VII.

*

The nativism that had long been associated with woman suffrage in the West may be seen not only in the speeches but in the voting of western congressmen. Typically, supporters of woman suffrage argued that native-born American women possessed a standard of morality that was either lacking or insufficiently developed in foreigners generally. As a Puritan crusade, woman suffrage was in many respects dedicated to the propositions that American politics was in

need of uplifting and that women were singularly
equipped to do the job. "Woman will raise the standard in
politics," declared Representative Campbell (R-Kans.),
"as she has raised and maintained the standard in every relation she sustains in life." [22] However, implicit in the ar-

TABLE VII

COMPARISON OF EAST AND WEST AYE VOTE ON
PROHIBITION AMENDMENT, DECEMBER 22, 1914

	East		West	
	%	Number	%	Number
All congressmen	28	181	57	135
Democrats	12	114	57	68
Republicans	46	57	54	56
Progressives	90	10	73	11
Rural	38	93	69	73
Urban	9	75	27	30
Mixed Rural and Urban	54	13	59	32

gument that the standards needed raising was the belief
that someone had lowered them. The woman suffrage supporters were usually fairly clear on who these people were.
In writing on the American electorate in 1904, the noted
suffragette Ida Husted Harper observed:

Consider what it [the electorate] has received during the
past thirty-five years from the majority of negroes, Indians
and immigrants who have been enfranchised during that
time, and then judge whether women as a body, could not
bring something to offset these last acquisitions. Those
who fear the foreign vote and the colored vote should remember that there are more native-born women in the
United States than foreign-born men and women; more
white women than colored men and women.[23]

This theme, of counterpoising a corrupted or at least corruptible electorate with the intelligence and virtue of

woman voters, occurs again and again in suffrage literature, for example, in the testimony of Representative Ed-
ward T. Taylor (D-Colo.) at a hearing on woman suffrage
in 1912, before the House Judiciary Committee:

> As there are one-third more girls than boys attending
> the high schools of this country, the women are very
> rapidly becoming the more educated. According to the
> last census, the illiterate men of this country very greatly
> outnumber the illiterate women. Therefore, extending
> the franchise to women will actually increase the propor-
> tion of intelligent voters. Moreover, extending the fran-
> chise to women will very greatly increase the number of
> native-born voters, because there are in the United States
> over twelve times as many native-born women as foreign
> born. It is also a matter of record that a less proportion of
> the foreign born than the native born vote, and, as there
> are much fewer women than men immigrants, the en-
> franchisement of women will therefore doubly tend to
> minimize the influence of the foreign vote.[24]

Yet this fear of the foreign vote, which the woman suffrage
supporters evidently capitalized upon, was not limited to
the suffrage camp. Fear of the foreigner was becoming an
important theme in American politics, and those opposed to
woman suffrage also tried to employ it to their advantage.
For example, in an article in the *North American Review*
in 1914, one opponent of woman suffrage stated: "Under
the proposed suffrage amendment the negro and Chinese
and Japanese women would soon be organized so as to
hold the balance of power in their states, as the Mormon
women really hold the balance of power in Utah, Colorado, and Idaho." [25] We can tell, however, which side of
the suffrage question benefited most from the nativist sen-

timent after we have analyzed the votes relevant to the issue.

In 1914, a vote on a literacy test requirement for immigration was taken in the 63rd Congress, which resulted in an overwhelming 239 in favor and 140 opposed. Simply stated, the literacy test requirement for immigration provided that persons 16 years of age or older had to be able to read and write some language to be eligible to enter the United States. Similar bills had previously drawn vetoes from Presidents Cleveland, Taft, and Wilson. The literacy test was a fairly undisguised form of restrictive and discriminatory legislation in that it favored immigrants from England and northwestern Europe, as was made quite clear by Senator Lodge (R-Mass.), an early advocate of the restriction. In a speech before the Senate in 1896, Lodge explained why he supported the measure.

The illiteracy test will bear most heavily upon the Italians, Russians, Poles, Hungarians, Greeks, and Asiatics, and very lightly, or not at all, upon English-speaking emigrants or Germans, Scandinavians, and French. In other words, the races most affected by the illiteracy test are those whose emigration to this country has begun within the last twenty years and swelled rapidly to enormous proportions, races with which the English-speaking people have never hitherto assimilated, and who are most alien to the great body of the people of the United States. On the other hand, immigrants from the United Kingdom and of those races which are most closely related to the English-speaking people, and who with the English-speaking people themselves founded the American colonies and built up the United States, are affected but little by the proposed test. . . . These kindred races also are those who alone go to the Western and

Southern States, where immigrants are desired, and take up our unoccupied lands. The races which would suffer most seriously by exclusion under the proposed bill furnish the immigrants who do not go to the West or South, where immigration is needed, but who remain on the Atlantic Seaboard, where immigration is not needed and where their presence is most injurious and undesirable.[26]

When the 63rd Congress passed a bill containing the literacy test restriction on immigration, President Wilson vetoed it with the observation that the bill substituted opportunity for character as a test of fitness. "Those who come seeking opportunity are not to be admitted unless they have already had one of the chief of the opportunities they seek, the opportunity of education. The object of such provisions is restriction, not selection." [27]

In addition to seeing the literacy test qualification for immigration as a substantive major change in our immigration policy, we may also see in it another of the symbolic conflicts over status in society. "When a society experiences profound changes," Joseph R. Gusfield has observed, "the fortunes and the respect of people undergo loss or gain. We have always understood the desire to defend fortune. We should also understand the desire to defend respect. It is less clear because it is symbolic in nature but it is not less significant." [28] Both substantively and symbolically, the literacy test restriction on immigration was the direct antecedent of the national origins system of immigration restriction of the 1920's. The groups favored under the literacy test—the English, Irish, and northwestern Europeans—were favored under the national origins system; and the groups discriminated against in the one case were discriminated against in the other. A vote in favor of the literacy test gave an improvement in status to immigrants from favored countries, as it gave a diminution of status to other immigrants. In the House vote of February 4, 1914, on the Burnett literacy test provision, the West supported the measure with 73 out of a possible 135 votes, or 54 per cent; the South gave 85 out of a possible 115 votes, or 74 per cent; while the East gave only 78 out of a possible 181 votes, or 43 per cent in favor of the test.

TABLE VIII

COMPARISON OF EAST AND WEST AYE VOTE ON LITERACY
TEST RESTRICTIONS, FEBRUARY 4, 1914

	East %	East Number	West %	West Number
All congressmen	43	181	54	135
Democrats	36	114	53	68
Republicans	51	57	50	56
Progressives	80	10	82	11
Rural	65	93	62	73
Urban	15	75	20	30
Mixed rural and urban	54	13	69	32

When we examine this vote from the point of view of party affiliation, we find that in the West 53 per cent of the Democrats supported the measure as did 50 per cent of the Republicans. In the South, 74 per cent of the Democrats voted in favor of it. In the East, however, only 36 per cent of the Democrats, but 51 per cent of the Republicans, supported the literacy test. The real division, of course, came with the conflict between the rural and urban districts. In the West, some 62 per cent of the rural congressmen of both parties favored the restriction, compared to only 20 per cent of the urban congressmen. In the East, nearly 65 per cent of the rural congressmen supported the literacy

test, compared to only 15 per cent of the urban congressmen. These results are summarized in Table VIII.[29]

As had been the case with the prohibition amendment,
the fundamental division over the literacy test provision
was essentially a conflict between rural, Puritan America
and urban, pluralistic America; and whether the issue was
liquor or immigration, rural America sought to prohibit
and restrict.

*

The obvious association of woman suffrage with prohibition and immigration restriction caused, however, a certain embarrassment to the woman suffrage leadership.
How could they recruit antiprohibition votes when one of
the major arguments in support of woman suffrage was
that it would lead to prohibition? How could they recruit
the naturalized American vote when one of the major
claims of the woman suffrage camp was that it would ensure political control by native-born Americans? As Aileen
S. Kraditor has reported, the eastern leadership of the
woman suffrage movement was aware of these difficulties.
As early as 1890, Susan B. Anthony wrote:

> The strongest argument to win the Prohibition men to
> vote for W.S.—is the very strongest one to drive from us
> the high license men.—So the strongest testimony showing
> how all women's voting will lessen the ratio of the foreign
> vote and of the Catholic vote—is just the worst thing—in
> fact wholly estops all hope of winning the foreign born
> men's vote—and the Catholic vote.—We are between two
> distracting dilemmas at every step. . . . But it is hardly
> possible to say anything—that will not hurt somebody—
> so each of us must be governed by our own true in-
> wardness—as to what and how to present our claims—.[30]

How then did the vote on these correlative values turn out in the 63rd Congress? Even when we set aside the South with its overwhelming vote against woman suffrage but for prohibition and the literacy test, great regional differences in the voting behavior appear. In the West, 86 per cent of the prohibition vote also supported woman suffrage, as did 84 per cent of the proliteracy test vote. On the other hand, 60 per cent of eastern prohibition supporters voted for woman suffrage, while 56 per cent of those opposed to prohibition were also opposed to woman suffrage. In the East, there was a nearly even distribution on the relation of the literacy test to woman suffrage; 42 per cent supported both, 44 per cent opposed both, and approximately 40 per cent divided no-yes (either way). However, it should be noted that in the East, 80 per cent of those favoring prohibition also supported the literacy test, while 62 per cent of the antiprohibition vote also opposed the literacy test. In the West, 74 per cent of the prohibitionists supported the literacy test, while 60 per cent of the antiprohibition vote opposed the literacy test.

Clearly, in the West the woman suffrage movement drew heavily upon a group that supported both prohibition and the literacy test. Indeed, the major opposition to woman suffrage in the West came from those who were against prohibition and the literacy test. In the East, on the other hand, it was evident that the woman suffrage movement by 1914 was appealing to a wider group. Eastern congressional support for woman suffrage was almost evenly divided among those for and against prohibition, and those for and against the literacy test. The major opposition to woman suffrage in the East, as in the West, came from those who opposed prohibition, generally representing urban districts.

*

In view of the voting record of the 63rd Congress, it is indeed remarkable that in the space of five years Congress could muster the necessary two-thirds majority to propose the prohibition and woman suffrage amendments, that the Puritan ethic which had been so clearly identified with the West should sweep through the South and East as well. The world war, no doubt, hastened this change, for the austerity and nativism implicit in Puritanism were re-emphasized under the protective cloak of patriotism. A vote in favor of the literacy test was also a vote against the eastern European allies of the Central Powers; in 1917, the year the United States entered the war, the Burnett literacy test bill was passed over President Wilson's second veto. A vote in favor of prohibition was also a vote against the German-American brewers of Milwaukee and St. Louis, as well as a vote in favor of the wartime conservation of sugar. In 1917, the eastern vote in favor of prohibition increased by nearly 68 per cent (from 59 to 99) to make possible the formal proposal of the Eighteenth Amendment. A vote in favor of woman suffrage was also a vote in favor of the "100% Americanism" that tended to characterize the last years of the Wilson regime. In 1919, the 66th Congress formally proposed the Nineteenth Amendment; in doing so it mustered a 100 per cent increase in favorable votes over the 63rd Congress in the East (from 72 to 145), a 357 per cent increase in the South (from 7 to 32), and a modest 34 per cent increase in the West (from 95 to 127). In August 1920, with the ratification of the Nineteenth Amendment by Tennessee, woman suffrage became part of the Constitution.

*

The first presidential election after the ratification of
the Nineteenth Amendment resulted in the overwhelming
victory of Warren G. Harding, who had offered the voters
a return to normalcy. As a symbolic appeal the return to
normalcy may be seen as connoting a postwar restoration
of the values of traditional America: of the primacy of the
small town, the middle class, the native-born, and the Protestant. This traditional ethos was reinforced by the one-
sided election of Calvin Coolidge, whom William Allen
White called "a Puritan in Babylon." It may be argued,
furthermore, that what Coolidge represented was the symbolic triumph of puritanism as the American norm, for all
that in actual politics and everyday life it was frequently
violated. It might be said that in the 1920's, "dry" America, "safe" from the immigrant influx, presented the image
of a Puritan Zion. Clearly this image of America was in
conflict with the reality of the direction of social change
and demographic movement that was actually taking
place. Industrialization and urbanization had been greatly
accelerated by World War I. The rural America that had
contained the majority of people in 1910 was shown by the
census of 1920 to have less population than urban America. It is not surprising, therefore, that Congress, aware of
the significance of this shift in population and what it portended in politics, did not reapportion itself (and consequently the electoral college) following the census of
1920. Presidents Harding, Coolidge, and Hoover were thus
elected by electoral colleges which were based upon appor-
tionments determined by the census of 1910. Not until the
election of 1932 was the electoral college brought up to

date again in its apportionment with the most recent census.

I am not arguing here that woman suffrage produced the victories of Harding, Coolidge, and Hoover, although doubtless it contributed to them. What I am arguing is that many of the men who voted for prohibition, woman suffrage, restrictive immigration, and Harding, Coolidge, and Hoover possessed an outlook, or shared a point of view, which governed in some measure their style of life and which I have subsumed here under the term "the Puritan ethic." Furthermore, I am not arguing that only because this point of view was so manifestly present in the West in particular could woman suffrage be enacted. Obviously, other combinations of attitudes and circumstances might at another time have led to the same results. Rather, I am saying that the best available evidence drawn from the politics of the issue supports the contention that the presence of the Puritan ethic in the West was a significant contributory factor to the rise of woman suffrage.

NOTES

INTRODUCTION

1. See James H. Timberlake, in his *Prohibition and the Progressive Movement, 1900–1920* (Cambridge: Harvard University Press, 1963), and Joseph R. Gusfield, in his *Symbolic Crusade: Status Politics and the American Temperance Movement* (Urbana: University of Illinois Press, 1963).

2. James H. Baker (ed.), *History of Colorado* (Denver: Linderman Co., Inc., 1927), Vol. I, p. 11.

3. Eleanor Flexner has done this in *Century of Struggle: The Woman's Rights Movement in the United States* (Cambridge: Harvard University Press, 1959), as has Andrew Sinclair in *The Better Half: The Emancipation of the American Woman* (New York: Harper & Row, Publishers, 1965).

4. Aileen S. Kraditor has published an excellent study of these in *The Ideas of the Woman Suffrage Movement, 1890–1920* (New York: Columbia University Press, 1965).

CHAPTER I

1. Saul K. Padover (ed.), *Thomas Jefferson on Democracy* (Baltimore: Penguin Books, Inc., 1946), p. 18.

2. George Bancroft, *Literary and Historical Miscellanies* (New York: Harper & Row, Publishers, 1855), p. 422.

3. Alexis de Tocqueville, *Democracy in America* (New York: Oxford University Press, 1947), p. 6.

4. *Ibid.*, p. 7.

5. *Ibid.*, p. 45.

6. *Ibid.*, p. 49.

7. *Ibid.*, p. 391.

8. *Ibid.*, p. 399.

9. *Ibid.*, p. 400.

10. Kirk H. Porter, *A History of Suffrage in the United States* (Chicago: The University of Chicago Press, 1918), p. 90.

11. *Ibid.*, pp. 234–5.

12. *Ibid.*, pp. 145, 227.

13. Carrie Chapman Catt and Nettie Rogers Shuler, *Woman Suffrage and Politics* (New York: Charles Scribner's Sons, 1923), p. 107.

14. Frederick Jackson Turner, *The Frontier in American History* (New York: Holt, Rinehart & Winston, Inc., 1962), pp. 243–4.

15. *Ibid.*, p. 259.

16. *Ibid.*, pp. 30–1.

17. *Ibid.*, p. 266.

18. Walter Prescott Webb, *The Great Plains* (Boston: Ginn and Company, 1931), p. vi.

19. See, for example: "American democracy was born of no theorist's dream; it was not carried in the *Sarah Constant* to Virginia, nor in the *Mayflower* to Plymouth. It came out of the American forest, and it gained new strength each time it touched a new frontier. Not the constitution, but free land and an abundance of natural resources open to a fit people, made the democratic type of society in America for three centuries while it occupied its empire." Turner, *op. cit.*, p. 293. In many of Turner's sentences not only is the frontier forested but abundant free land is good farming terrain. Neither condition typically existed in Webb's West.

20. Webb, *op. cit.* p. vi.

21. *Ibid.*, p. 428.

22. *Ibid.*, p. 246.

23. *Ibid.*, p. 509. And also, "The West, or the Great Plains, presents also a survival of the early American stock, the so-called typical American of English or Scotch and Scotch-Irish descent."

24. *Ibid.*, p. 248.

25. *Ibid.*, p. 505.

26. Tocqueville, *op. cit.*, pp. 187–8.

27. I am arguing here that what has been called frontier equalitarianism might be more accurately termed white man's equalitarianism, as in general it held no brief for equality of sexes or races. David M. Potter's *People of Plenty* (Chicago: The University of Chicago Press, 1954), which interprets the frontier thesis as one of abundance, notes its limitation to Anglo-Americans. For example, "In short, abundance is partly a physical and partly a cultural manifestation. For America, from the eighteenth to the twentieth century, the frontier was the focus of abundance, physically because the land there was virgin and culturally because the Anglo-Americans of that time were particularly apt at exploiting the new country. At this lowest threshold of access to abundance the pioneers found an individualism and a nationalism which they might not have found at other thresholds. . . . The frontier remained of primary significance precisely as long as it remained the lowest thresh-

old of access to America's abundance; it ceased to be primary when other thresholds were made lower, and not when the edge of unsettled land ceased to exist." Pp. 164–5.

28. See Eleanor Flexner, *Century of Struggle: The Woman's Rights Movement in the United States* (Cambridge: Harvard University Press, 1959); Catt and Shuler, *op. cit.*

29. Marion Mills Miller (ed.), *Great Debates in American History* (New York: Current Literature Publishing Company, 1913), Vol. VIII, pp. 26–7.

CHAPTER II

1. In *Senate Report No. 70, 49th Congress, 1st Session,* Select Committee on Woman Suffrage (Feb. 2, 1886), p. 4.

2. See Eleanor Flexner, *Century of Struggle: The Woman's Rights Movement in the United States* (Cambridge: Harvard University Press, 1959); Andrew Sinclair, *The Better Half* (New York: Harper & Row, Publishers, 1965); Leonard J. Arrington, *Great Basin Kingdom* (Cambridge: Harvard University Press, 1958); Richard Vetterli, *Mormonism, Americanism and Politics* (Salt Lake City: Ensign Publishing Company, 1961); Irving Stone, *Men to Match My Mountains* (Garden City, N.Y.: Doubleday & Company, Inc., 1956); Earl S. Pomeroy, *The Pacific Slope* (New York: Alfred A. Knopf, Inc. 1965).

3. Cited by William Mulder, *Homeward to Zion: The Mormon Migration From Scandinavia* (Minneapolis: University of Minnesota Press, 1957), p. 315.

4. Arrington, *op. cit.*, p. 3.

5. C. C. Goodwin, "The Mormon Situation," *Harper's Magazine,* 63 (Oct. 1881) 760.

6. "Memorial Adopted by Citizens of Salt Lake City, Utah Territory," Mar. 31, 1870, against H. R. Number 1089, the Cullom bill, *Senate Miscellaneous Document Number 112,* 41st Congress, 2nd Session, p. 1.

7. Stone, *op. cit.*, p. 220.

8. Orson Spencer, *Patriarchial Order* (Liverpool: S. W. Richards, 1853), p. 2, cited in Vetterli, *op. cit.*, p. 481.

9. Arrington, *op. cit.*, p. 63.

10. Stone, *op. cit.*, p. 218.

11. *Ibid.*, p. 226.

12. Vetterli, *op. cit.*, p. 592

13. Petition of Mrs. Angie F. Newman on "Woman Suffrage in Utah," June 8, 1886, *Senate Miscellaneous Document No. 122,* 49th Congress, 1st Session, pp. 3, 5.

14. Marion Mills Miller (ed.), *Great Debates in American History*

(New York: Current Literature Publishing Company, 1913), Vol. VIII, pp. 26–7.

15. Petition of Mrs. Angie F. Newman, *op. cit.*, p. 2.

16. Cited in Arrington, *op. cit.*, p. 255.

17. Stone, *op. cit.*, p. 192.

18. Cited in Arrington, *op. cit.*, p. 481.

19. Quoted in Vetterli, *op. cit.*, p. 545.

20. See "Abstract of Returns of an Election Held in Utah Territory on March 18, 1872 for the purpose of voting for or against the Constitution of the proposed State of Deseret," *Senate Miscellaneous Document Number 126*, 42nd Congress, 2nd Session, p. 1.

21. Petition of Mrs. Angie F. Newman, *op. cit.*, p. 3.

22. *Ibid.*

23. Goodwin, *op. cit.*, p. 760.

24. Petition of Mrs. Angie F. Newman, *op. cit.*, p. 4.

25. *Ibid.*, p. 5.

26. *Ibid.*, p. 8.

27. *Ibid.*, p. 1.

28. Andrew Love Neff, *History of Utah, 1847 to 1869* (Salt Lake City: Leland Hargrave Creer, 1940), p. 109.

29. Alexander Evanoff, "The Turner Thesis and Mormon Beginnings in New York and Utah," *Utah Historical Quarterly, 33* (1965) 170.

30. Hubert Howe Bancroft, *History of Utah* (San Francisco: The History Company, Publishers, 1889), p. 394.

31. Cited in Vetterli, *op. cit.*, p. 635.

32. According to M. R. Werner, *Brigham Young* (New York: Harcourt, Brace & World, Inc., 1925), the women did vote as expected, as did their husbands, "thus forming a powerful political advantage of the Mormon Church in Utah." p. 364.

33. Vetterli, *op. cit.*, p. 659.

34. Stewart Lofgren Grow, *The Utah Commission*. Unpublished Doctoral Thesis, University of Utah, 1954, p. 50, as cited in Vetterli, *op. cit.*, pp. 673–4.

35. Cited in Vetterli, *op. cit.*, p. 688.

36. Richard D. Poll, "A State is Born," *Utah Historical Quarterly, 32* (1964) 19.

37. Stanley S. Ivins, "A Constitution for Utah," *Utah Historical Quarterly,* 25 (1957) 95–106.

Chapter III

1. Louis B. Wright, *Culture on the Moving Frontier* (New York: Harper & Row, Publishers, 1961), p. 132.

2. *Wyoming* (W.P.A. American Guide Series), (New York: Oxford University Press, 1941), p. 72.

3. *Ibid.*, p. 186.

4. Quoted in Struthers Burt, *Powder River* (New York: Farrar, Straus & Giroux, 1938), pp. 145–6.

5. *Wyoming, op. cit.*, p. 197.

6. Marie H. Erwin, *Wyoming Historical Blue Book* (Denver: Bradford–Robinson Printing Co., 1943) , p. 163.

7. Susan B. Anthony, *History of Woman Suffrage* (Rochester, N.Y.: Charles Mann, 1887), Vol. III, p. 747.

8. See *Blue Book, op. cit.*, p. 362.

9. *Ibid.*, p. 529.

10. Cited in Eleanor Flexner, *Century of Struggle* (Cambridge: Harvard University Press, 1959), p. 354.

11. Catt and Shuler, *Woman Suffrage and Politics* (New York: Charles Scribner's Sons, 1923), pp. 75–6.

12. Anthony, *op. cit.*, Vol. III, p. 730.

13. Address of Governor John W. Hoyt, of Wyoming Territory, "Upon Woman Suffrage in Wyoming," delivered at Association Hall, Philadelphia, April 3, 1882, p. 8. Portions of this are also printed in Anthony, *op. cit.*, Vol. III, p. 730.

14. Andrew Sinclair, *The Better Half: The Emancipation of the American Woman* (New York: Harper & Row, Publishers, 1965), p. 209.

15. Hoyt, *op. cit.*, pp. 8–9.

16. My italics. Anthony, *op. cit.*, Vol. III, p. 730. As evidence of Mr. W.H. Bright's sincerity in the cause of woman suffrage it may be noted that in Denver, Colorado, in 1877, Mr. Bright spoke at an equal-rights meeting and served on a committee in support of woman suffrage in the referendum held in Colorado that year. *Ibid.*, p. 722.

17. *Ibid.*, pp. 730–31. Mrs. Anthony noted that after Justices Howe and Kingman left Governor Campbell, Mrs. M. B. Arnold and Mrs. Amalia B. Post saw him, "urging him to sign the bill on the highest moral grounds; not only to protect the personal rights of the women of the territory *but to compel the men to observe the decencies of life and to elevate the social and political status of the people.*" *Ibid.* My italics. Andrew Sinclair, *op. cit.*, writes that Governor Campbell "was also married to a suffragist." p. 209. Catt and Shuler, *op. cit.*, p. 78, noted that Governor Campbell was unmarried.

18. Anthony, *op. cit.*, p. 731.

19. *Ibid.*

20. *Ibid.*, p. 734.

21. *Ibid.*, p. 735. My italics.

22. *Ibid.*, p. 736.

23. *Ibid.*, p. 737.

24. *Ibid.*, p. 736. By the 1880's the practice of calling women jurors was abandoned.

25. Aliens who had declared their intentions of becoming U.S. citizens were, along with citizens, elegible to vote if they were resident in the territory at the time.

26. Until 1880 the legislature was elected in odd years.

27. In the 1870 Census, Laramie County had an adult male population of 1877.

28. This table is collated from various tallies given in the Wyoming *Blue Book, op. cit.*

29. My italics. Anthony, *op. cit.*, pp. 738–9. In the 1869 election in South Pass City, a Negro who sought to vote had been beaten up by "some drunken fellows with large knives and loaded revolvers." According to Kingman, "There were quite a number of colored men who wanted to vote, but did not dare approach the polls until the United States Marshal placed himself at their head and with revolver in hand escorted them through the crowd, saying he would shoot the first man that interfered with them. There was much quarreling and tumult, but the negroes voted." *Ibid.*, p. 729.

30. *Ibid.*, p. 739. My italics.

31. Wright, *op. cit.*, p. 168.

32. *Ibid.*, pp. 196–7.

33. *Blue Book, op. cit.*, pp. 259–64.

34. Wright, *op. cit.*, p. 238.

35. Anthony, *op. cit.*, Vol. III, p. 740.

36. Voting throughout was not, therefore, along straight party lines as reported by Justice Kingman. See *Ibid.*, p. 741.

37. Frances Parkman, *The Oregon Trail* (New York: Mentor Books, 1950), p. 129.

CHAPTER IV

1. Susan B. Anthony and Ida Husted Harper, *The History of Woman Suffrage* (Rochester, N.Y.: Susan B. Anthony, 1902), Vol. IV, p. xiii.

2. *Ibid.*, p. xiv.

3. *Ibid.*, p. xvii.

4. *Ibid.*, p. xviii.

5. *Ibid.*, p. 437.

6. *Idem.*

7. *Ibid.,* p. 438.

8. *Ibid.,* pp. 438–9.

9. *Ibid.,* p. xix.

10. *Idem.*

11. *Idem.*

12. *Ibid.,* p. 534.

13. *Ibid.,* p. xix.

14. *Ibid.,* p. 1046.

15. *Ibid.,* pp. 1046–7.

16. *Ibid.,* p. 492.

17. *Ibid.,* p. 556.

18. *Ibid.,* p. xxi.

19. "Arguments of the Woman-Suffrage Delegates before the Committee on the Judiciary of the United States Senate, January 23, 1880," *Senate Miscellaneous Document No. 74,* 47th Congress, 1st Session, pp. 25–6.

20. Anthony and Harper, *op. cit.,* Vol. IV, p. 515.

21. *Ibid.,* Vol. III, p. 717.

22. *Ibid.,* Vol. IV, p. 896.

23. *Ibid.,* p. 500.

24. *Ibid.,* p. 493.

25. *Ibid.,* pp. 493–4.

26. *Ibid.,* Vol. III, p. 724.

27. *Ibid.,* Vol. IV, p. xxii.

28. *Ibid.,* p. xxii.

29. *Ibid.,* p. xxvi.

30. *Ibid.,* p. 593.

31. *Ibid.,* pp. 517–18.

32. *Ibid.,* p. 518.

33. Frederick Jackson Turner, "Dominant Forces in Western Life," in *The Frontier in American History* (New York: Holt, Rinehart & Winston, Inc., 1962), pp. 239–40.

34. Carrie Chapman Catt and Nettie Rogers Shuler, *Woman Suffrage and Politics* (New York: Charles Scribner's Sons, 1923), p. 162. Italics in original.

CHAPTER V

1. V. O. Key, Jr., and Winston W. Crouch, *The Initiative and Referendum in California* (Berkeley: University of California Press, 1939), p. 426.

2. *Ibid.,* p. 427.

3. *Ibid.,* p. 432.
4. *Ibid.,* p. 440.
5. Ida Husted Harper (ed.), *The History of Woman Suffrage* (National American Woman Suffrage Association, 1922), Vol. VI, p. 50.
6. For the initative and referendum: South Dakota (1898), Utah (1900), Oregon (1902), Nevada (referendum 1904, initiative 1912), Montana (1906), Oklahoma (1907), Maine (1908), Missouri (1908), Michigan (1908), Arkansas (1910), Colorado (1910), California (1911), New Mexico (1911), Arizona (1911), Idaho (1912), Nebraska (1912), Ohio (1912), Washington (1912). For the recall: Oregon (1908), California (1911), Arizona (1912), Idaho (1912), Washington (1912), Colorado (1912), Nevada (1912), Michigan (1913), Louisiana (1914), North Dakota (1914), Kansas (1914). Harold V. Faulkner, *The Quest for Social Justice, 1898–1914* (New York: The Macmillan Company, 1931), pp. 85–6.
7. Richard Hofstadter, *The Age of Reform* (New York: Random House, Inc., 1960), p. 135.
8. *Ibid.,* pp. 150, 152.
9. George E. Mowry, *The Era of Theodore Roosevelt* (New York: Harper & Row, Publishers, 1962) , p. 51.
10. *Ibid.,* pp. 35–6.
11. Faulkner, *op. cit.,* p. 21.
12. Hofstadter, *op. cit.,* p. 83.
13. Mowry, *op. cit.,* p. 93.
14. John Higham, *Strangers in the Land* (New York: Atheneum Publishers, 1963), pp. 150–51.
15. *Historical Statistics of the United States, Colonial Times to 1957* (Washington, D.C.: U.S. Government Printing Office, 1960), p. 66.
16. Higham, *op. cit.,* p. 168.
17. Gilman M. Ostrander, *The Prohibition Movement in California, 1848–1933* (Berkeley: University of California Press, 1957), p. 63.
18. Higham, *op. cit.,* p. 365.
19. *Ibid.,* p. 169.
20. C. Vann Woodward, *The Strange Career of Jim Crow* (New York: Oxford University Press, 1966), p. 19.
21. Alan P. Grimes, *Equality in America* (New York: Oxford University Press, 1964), p. 55.
22. Josiah Strong, *Our Country* (New York: Baker & Taylor, 1885), p. 175.
23. James H. Timberlake, *Prohibition and the Progressive Move-*

ment, 1900–1920 (Cambridge: Harvard University Press, 1963), pp. 5–6.

24. *Ibid.,* pp. 32–3.

25. Peter H. Odegard, *Pressure Politics: The Story of the Anti-Saloon League* (New York: Columbia University Press, 1928), p. 17.

26. See Ostrander, *op. cit.,* pp. 102–3.

27. *Ibid.,* p. 116.

28. Timberlake, *op. cit.,* pp. 2, 29–30.

29. Aileen Kraditor, *The Ideas of the Woman Suffrage Movement, 1890–1920* (New York: Columbia University Press), 1965), p. 57.

30. Harper, *op. cit.,* Vol. VI, p. 543.

31. *Ibid.,* p. 680.

32. In 1914, Washington, Oregon, Colorado, Arizona; in 1915, Idaho; in 1916, Montana; in 1917, Utah. Timberlake, *op. cit.,* p. 166.

33. *Ibid.,* p. 2.

34. *Ibid.,* p. 166.

35. Harper, *op. cit.,* Vol. VI. p. 377.

36. *Ibid.,* p. 510.

37. *Ibid.,* p. 503.

38. Mabel Craft Deering, "The Women's Demonstrations," *Collier Weekly,* 48 (Jan. 6, 1912) 18.

CHAPTER VI

1. For purposes of this and the following tables, the West includes Arizona, California, Colorado, Idaho, Illinois, Iowa, Kansas, Minnesota, Missouri, Montana, Nebraska, Nevada, New Mexico, North Dakota, Oklahoma, Oregon, South Dakota, Utah, Washington, Wisconsin, Wyoming. The South includes Alabama, Arkansas, Florida, Georgia, Louisiana, Mississippi, North Carolina, South Carolina, Tennessee, Texas, Virginia. The East includes Connecticut, Delaware, Indiana, Kentucky, Maine, Maryland, Massachusetts, Michigan, New Hampshire, New Jersey, New York, Ohio, Pennsylvania, Rhode Island, Vermont, West Virginia. Senate vote reported in *Congressional Record,* Vol. 51, Part V, p. 5108 (63rd Congress, 2nd Session, Mar. 19, 1914).

2. Vote reported in *Congressional Record,* Vol. 52, Part II, pp. 1483–4 (63rd Congress, 3rd Session, Jan. 12, 1915).

3. Aileen S. Kraditor, *The Ideas of the Woman Suffrage Movement, 1890–1920* (New York: Columbia University Press, 1965), p. 166.

4. Carrie Chapman Catt and Nettie Rogers Shuler, *Woman Suffrage and Politics* (New York: Charles Scribner's Sons, 1923), p. 147.

5. *Congressional Record,* Vol. 51, Part V, p. 4962.

6. *Ibid.* (May 19, 1914), p. 5101.

7. *Ibid.,* p. 5103.

8. *Ibid.,* p. 5097.

9. *Ibid.,* pp. 5093–4.

10. *Ibid.,* p. 5104.

11. *Ibid.,* Vol. 52, Part II, pp. 1413–14.

12. *Ibid.,* p. 1421.

13. *Harper's Weekly,* 53 (1909) 5.

14. *The New York Times,* Jan. 6, 1915, p. 15.

15. Anna Howard Shaw, "Equal Suffrage—A Problem of Political Justice," *Annals of the American Academy of Political and Social Science,* 56 (1914) 97.

16. *Congressional Record,* Vol. 51 Part V, p. 5088.

17. James H. Timberlake, *Prohibition and the Progressive Movement, 1900–1920* (Cambridge: Howard University Press, 1963), p. 166.

18. *Ibid.,* p. 163.

19. Joseph Gusfield, *Symbolic Crusade: Status Politics and the American Temperance Movement* (Urbana: University of Illinois Press, 1963), pp. 7–8.

20. *America,* 11, No. 5 (May 16, 1914) 119; 12, No. 14 (Jan. 16, 1915) 351.

21. *Congressional Record,* Vol. 52, Part I, p. 616, for prohibition vote of December 22, 1914.

22. *Congressional Record,* Vol. 52, Part II, p. 1409 (January 12, 1915).

23. Ida Husted Harper, "Would Woman Suffrage Benefit the State, and Woman Herself?" *North American Review,* 178 (1904) 373.

24 Marion M. Miller (ed.), *Great Debates in American History* (New York: Current Literature Publishing Co., 1913), Vol. 8, p. 370.

25. Molly Elliott Seawell, "Two Suffrage Mistakes," *North American Review,* 199 (1914) 373.

26. Excerpted in Edith Abbott (ed.), *Immigration: Select Documents and Case Records* (Chicago: University of Chicago Press, 1924), pp. 193–4.

27. Cited in *Ibid.,* p. 215.

28. Gusfield, *op. cit.,* p. 11.

29. *Congressional Record,* Vol. 51, Part III, pp. 2910–11, for vote.

30. Kraditor, *op. cit.,* p. 57–8.

DATE DUE